THE POLITICAL ELITE IN ARGENTINA

THE POLITICAL ELITE

IN ARGENTINA

JULIO A. FERNÁNDEZ
University of Colorado

With a Foreword by Russell H. Fitzgibbon

New York: NEW YORK UNIVERSITY PRESS
1970

© 1970 by New York University
Library of Congress Catalog Card Number 77-133015
SBN 0-8147-2551-1
Manufactured in the United States of America

To Doris

61790

CONTENTS

FOREWORD

Just recently in the United States, as this is written, we have witnessed the recurrent search for political talent to fill a large number of top policy-making, administrative posts as a new national administration and a different party have come into power. To some degree, the phenomenon is observable every four years—and of course in part is continuous—but when a change of party control occurs simultaneously with the coming of a new occupant to the White House, the hunt for able persons to staff the multitude of positions is necessarily dramatized, expanded, and intensified.

There are very few modern states, even those of small population and simple organization, in which some degree of systematization has not been introduced into the recruitment process for filling governmental positions. Gone are the days (to set the problem in an Argentine context) when the appointments to high government posts could be made as casually or unsystematically as under a Rosas or even a Mitre or a Sarmiento. Even during the unlamented days over the middle of this century, when virtually the sole qualification for appointment or advancement was to be a good *Peronista,* the Government had to have some procedures for systematization in manning the prostituted public service.

We have come to have a reasonably good picture of the general outlines of the government and politics of the several Latin American states, but it is a picture painted in broad brush strokes with many details not filled in. Even for an advanced state such as Argentina, the number of serious and professional published studies advancing our particularized understanding of the anatomy, physiology, and psychology of the body politic could probably be counted on the fingers of one hand.

The situation is much the same with regard to elective office. The filling of such positions is more dramatic and spotlighted than is the recruitment of persons for the administrative bureaucracy, but it yields to many of the same elements of conditioning; and it has been insufficiently studied, either in Argentina or elsewhere in Latin America.

Professor Fernández turns his attention in this outstanding study of political elites in Argentina to just those aspects which have traditionally needed more light directed toward them. He has set himself to examine certain phases and appearances of recruitment and particular attitudes of the elites in the political process in that important South American state.

It is fortunate that he was enabled to undertake field research for his study during an interlude of civilian and democratic control. The relatively tortured political history of Argentina in the past quarter of a century has had its years when investigation of the kind here represented would have been impossible or unrewarding, but the administrations of Presidents Frondizi and Illia probably reflected the political process at its freest. It was a relative matter: the shadow of the military was never absent, and of course at the end of each of those two constitutional periods it completely eclipsed civilianism. If the regime of President Onganía continues for some time it will prove ultimately impossible to make a further study of this kind for the period on which Professor Fernández has focused. Hence, we are the more in his debt for having salvaged, while they were still salvageable, the data from which he draws his conclusions. He has given us a study which will long have relevance for the Argentine political scene.

Russell H. Fitzgibbon

University of California
Santa Barbara

AUTHOR'S NOTE

The simple purpose of this book is to add my small contribution to our understanding of the political leadership in a country whose prospects for political integration and stability remain dim but not hopeless. With the hope of shedding some light on the difficult processes of Argentine politics, I have set for myself the task of examining selected aspects of the political elite in Argentina, specifically their recruitment tendencies and attitudinal patterns.

What follows is not intended to be an exhaustive discourse upon elite theory; but is more concerned with the functional as opposed to the ideological utility of the term "elite" for inquiring into variables associated with leadership in Argentina.

The time period of this study is 1958 through 1965, based on the constitutional administrations of President Arturo Frondizi (1958–1962) and Arturo Illia (1963–1966). Using a total population of 398 and 384 office holders respectively for the 1958 and 1963 administrations, comparisons were made between the two governments with regard to certain determined variables of recruitment. The hypothesis of the presence of cohesive nationalism among the political elite toward specific issues is examined through the use of an attitude questionnaire administered to a sample of the Argentine political elite. This questionnaire represents my pioneer attempt to construct such an instrument in the Spanish vernacular; thus limitations as to the reliability and validity of the items selected are acknowledged. It is hoped that the observations made, however tentative, will provide valuable insights and stimulate further inquiry.

Research for this study was carried out in Buenos Aires over a four-month period. Biographical information was gathered from various sources including interviews, the Archives of the National Congress, *Quien es Quien en la Argentina* (the Argentine *Who's Who*), the library of the Ministry of the Interior, and newspapers for the period under study. The attitude questionnaire was administered by interview and mail. The operational procedures employed in the investigation were conditioned by the existing limitations of time and the general problem of accessibility attending field work in a Latin country—which at the time was on the threshold of a military coup.

For the realization of this endeavor, there are several persons to whom a debt of gratitude is due. I am especially grateful to former presidents Arturo Illia, Arturo Frondizi, and Pedro Aramburu who were kind enough to see me and to clarify various issues. I am also indebted to various Argentine friends and political leaders, many of whom must remain anonymous, but to whom I owe a great deal for their stimulating discussions.

To Professor Russell H. Fitzgibbon, my professor, mentor, and friend, I owe a very deep debt of gratitude for his advice and encouragement. I am also grateful to the many specialists on Argentine politics whose works have helped to clarify my thinking on the innumerable problems that have plagued Argentina. I am further indebted to my colleagues Professors Edward Rozek and Dayton McKean who read the manuscript and offered valuable suggestions. I alone, however, am responsible for the presentation, interpretations, and observations contained herein. Financial assistance for the project was provided through fellowships from the University of California and the Organization of American States.

J.A.F.

THE POLITICAL ELITE IN ARGENTINA

CHAPTER 1

THE THEORETICAL SETTING

This book centers on the functional as opposed to the ideological utility of the term "elite" [1] for inquiring into variables associated with political leadership in Argentina. It is worth noting that this key concept, "the elite," has ideological connotations as well as analytical value, and it may be well to examine briefly its controversial side before commenting on the development of the term as an analytical tool.

The consideration that makes the position of the ideological elitist so controversial is the moral argument for rule by the few. This does not apply to the use of the concept as an analytical tool for empirical research since the latter has nothing to do with the moral question of "what should be."

ELITE: THE IDEOLOGICAL SIDE

The ideological argument is cogently made that elitism—by definition the belief that a special few should rule—must be accepted because it is impossible to avoid such a political leadership arrangement in society. This position was developed elaborately by Vilfredo Pareto, Gaetano Mosca, and Roberto Michels

1

in the twentieth century. What was suggested was that the lower stratum, or the many in society, never stand a chance of achieving positions of leadership because the few will inevitably prevail in exercising the role of governance in every society no matter what its form.

It should be stressed that this eminent school of Italian theorists suggests that the very idea of democracy would seem incompatible with the idea of elites.[2] The notion of the indispensable, logical, and oligarchic character points up the element of inequality which may be present between the many who are ruled and the few who do the ruling.

One may question whether it is possible to concentrate political power in the hands of a few without destroying the principle of equality characteristic of a democratic order. Michels suggests that organization itself in either a developed or developing system where individuals interact would lead to the emergence of a rule-making minority who would bear the brunt of all decision-making for the rest. The ethical question that remains is concerned with the representativeness and accountability of this sector in relation to that societal segment that is being ruled.

There is the opposing theory that it is possible for the few to rule the many because the many can be persuaded of the moral superiority of the rulers. For instance, various forms of propaganda and techniques of indoctrination may be used in some countries to shape the minds, affections and beliefs of those ruled. It is possible to observe in modern polities the social engineering of deep attachments and almost servile dependence of the ruled toward contemporary political dictators or *caudillos*, event-making men, or military-backed rulers. Examples are the reverence given to Marxism-Leninism in the U.S.S.R., Nasserism in Egypt, Fidelism in Cuba, and Peronism in Argentina. Not to be overlooked is the alleged association of this ideological concept of the elite with the Fascist precepts of racialism and imperialism, inequality and violence which fail to jibe with the normative aspects of democracy.[3] Nor should it be overlooked that the many in society can be persuaded of some kind of superiority of leaders—not necessarily moral; the belief may be simply in their expertise to assume and carry out the responsibilities of governance effectively.

Valuable insight into the fallacy of Mosca, Pareto, and Michels is best pointed up by Sidney Hook who makes it clear that "so far as the position of these social philosophers is based on the constancy of human nature, their entire political wisdom consists in framing a simple alternative to man—rule or be ruled!" [4] Indeed the democratic theory of government, while it does not claim perfection, is in practice realizable to the extent that one is willing to strive for its workability.

ELITES: THE SCIENTIFIC SIDE

From the standpoint of scientific research it is assumed that in most societies there exists an observable pattern in which high social status is closely related to recruitment to high political office and/or access to the occupants of such offices. The major question then becomes whether there seems to occur a high degree of circulation among holders of key decision-making posts. In this regard, it may be important to inquire among those who govern not only whether there is willingness or capacity to assimilate but also whether there is willingness or capacity to destroy individuals seeking entrance into the elite. To this end, one might also ask whether those who become members of the political class are less bent than nonmembers on legitimizing their class in the sense of winning support from the outside. It may be that some endeavor to provide justification for the political elite sector merely by persuading the broad social strata that, whether by natural selection or political election, they do in fact possess the qualities to govern the rest (the majority) effectively with the maximum cooperation from the latter.

Various kinds of *coups d'état,* when they succeed, may operate for assimilation purposes in that they transfer the reins of government from one group of office-holders to a similar group. This group often seeks office as an opening wedge into society's upper circle of families, as in the case of the successful military officer who has risen from humble beginnings. "Palace revolutions" often fall into this category, and so do many "revolutions" in Latin America that eject one dictator only to put another one in without any real consequence for the stratification arrangement.

It should be pointed out that there are methodological difficulties in any effort to apply the elitist concept systematically. One must recognize that there may be various categories of political influence and diverse groups associated with such types of influence. Thus the locus of power must be recognized as elusive and often plural rather than singular in countries still undergoing the processes of change.

ELITE RECRUITMENT

Among some of the ideas germane to research procedure dealing with leadership and elite recruitment in such developing systems as Argentina, it is helpful to keep in mind the following: First, it is important to discuss the manner in which the elite are recruited and their relations to the nonelite; second, if the research objective is to show that elite groups exercise political leadership it may be also important to determine whether the elite control the channels of recruitment and whether they are able to mobilize support and acceptance of their values; third, recruitment should be understood as one of the essential input functions of any political system.[5]

The concern of this particular book is with an essentially multiparty system, sometimes styled "immobilist," in which, by definition, political parties have been unable to function with any degree of continuity in effective electoral competition. From the standpoint of decision-making, the following relevant questions may be raised: How are the political or decision-making elite selected; and what is the composition of the political elite? These questions are essential to providing data and hypotheses for cross-national comparative analysis of political systems.

Of special importance are styles in the political recruitment process which also have significance for the composition of elites. A distinction must be made between ascriptive and performance criteria as employed in recruitment. It may be, for example, that even in the most modern political system there will be a mixture of both ascription and performance or achievement criteria in the political selection process. The point to note, however, in contrasting the more modern with the less developed or less modern system is the relative weight assigned to achievement vis-à-vis personalistic factors in the process of political selection. Thus a person's level of education and formal record of achievement may determine his "availability" for recruitment into the political elite to a greater or less degree.[6]

Not to be overlooked are certain common-sense hypotheses which extend the field of inquiry for the study of elites in developing systems. First, persons who have high decision-making posts on the basis of ascription constitute a self-perpetuating group. Second, persons oriented toward modernization who attain leadership in the "liberal elite" are recruited from professional and middle classes. Third, training at universities in more developed countries coincides with a favorable view toward modernization in the home country. Fourth, persons recruited into the political elite who have an authoritarian bias ("guided democracy" type) are from professional and middle classes and only a few from the aristocracy. Finally, radical leadership is recruited from those who identify themselves as intellectuals, regardless of social origin.[7]

ELITE ATTITUDES

Research on a number of variables in relation to the elite such as legitimacy, accountability, representativeness, skills, and educational qualifications for governance can provide a basis for inferences with respect to the quality of elite performance in the political process of resolving issues and demands. Attitudinal perspectives of the decision-making elite in connection with these variables are also of paramount importance if field research has made data available.[8]

The importance of assessing the implicit values and beliefs of a political elite in a modernizing situation cannot be overstressed. Neither can the inherent limitations attending measurement of attitudes be overlooked. Everett Hagen has pointed out that the elite in the less modern or more traditional societies tend to have a much different world outlook, far different motivations, and a stronger sense of their own identity as the elite than do members of middle and upper classes from whom political leaders are more frequently recruited in the modern industrial society.[9] On an empirical basis it is difficult, however, to pinpoint attitudes as such, to differentiate their specificity, to assess their durability in any point in time, and to isolate the political socialization process or processes responsible for attitudinal changes in the elites.[10]

In this book some of the extant elite theories will be applied to the case of Argentina. The data to be presented here shed light on the aspects of selection and attitudes of the political elite in that country. It is assumed the selection process may add to our understanding of trends in the channels of access to political power during the periods of constitutional order in this major Latin American country; similarly, the attitudinal patterns may inspire policy-oriented analysis and new patterns of behavior relevant to a modernizing system. Political attitudes are a product of experiences derived from political socialization (or the deliberate shaping of attitudes in a citizenry) which bear direct relation to the process of leadership selection.[11]

NOTES

1. Literature on elite studies has grown tremendously in recent years. The reader may wish to consult some of the following references which are to be found in the Bibliography: Agger, Goldrich, and Swanson, *The Rulers and the Ruled;* Bell, *Jamaican Leaders;* Bottomore, *Elites and Society;* Beck, Malloy, and Campbell, *A Survey of Elite Studies;* de Imaz, *Los Que Mandan;* Lasswell and Lerner, eds., *World Revolutionary Elites;* Lipset and Solari, eds., *Elites in Latin America;* Meisel, *The Myth of the Ruling Class;* Michels, *Political Parties;* Mills, ed., *Images of Man;* Mosca, *The Ruling Class;* Pareto, *The Mind and Society*.

2. In his critique of Mosca, Pareto, and Michels, the author leans heavily on the discussion of Professor Sidney Hook in his book, *The Hero in History*, pp. 240–245.

3. See Ebenstein, *Great Political Thinkers,* pp. 589–600.

4. Hook, *op. cit.,* p. 245.

5. Cf. Scoble, "Leadership Hierarchies and Political Issues in a New England Town," in *Community Political Systems,* p. 122. Also see Almond, "Introduction," in *The Politics of the Developing Areas,* pp. 31–32.

6. Almond, *op. cit.,* p. 32.

7. For an explanation of the terms "traditional," "liberal," "authoritarian," and "radical," see Macridis and Brown, eds., *Comparative Politics,* pp. 433–434.

8. Lasswell, Lerner, and Rothwell, *The Comparative Study of Elites,* p. 6.

9. Hagen, *On the Theory of Social Change,* p. 75.

10. Singer, "Cosmopolitan Attitudes and International Relations Courses," pp. 318–319.

11. See Prewitt, "Political Socialization and Leadership Selection," pp. 96–111.

CHAPTER 2

POLITICAL LEADERSHIP
IN ARGENTINA

No problem is more critical to the success or failure of a society's process of democratization than that of attracting a broad enough leadership to provide some sense of stability and continuity to the political process. Argentina, unlike other more advanced underdeveloped societies, has been virtually unable to effect the peaceful transfer of power in any durable form through elections without undue recourse to *golpe de estado.*

This pattern of atomization and instability has characterized Argentine political life since its achievement of independence.[1] Even prior to independence there was marked instability within the country manifested by the existing antagonism between the *porteños* (the inhabitants of Buenos Aires) and the *provincianos* (the people of the interior). In 1812, with General Belgrano leading its army, Argentina defeated the Spaniards, making way for the Congress of Tucumán, which in July 1816 proclaimed Argentina's independence from Spain.

A NEW NATION'S LEADERSHIP

The delegates in attendance at the Congress of Tucumán signed the declaration of independence and named the royalist Juan Martín Pueyrredón supreme director; they then set about searching for a king. However, the *caudillos* (political bosses) of the interior were opposed to all royalist projects, and when in 1819 Pueyrredón and his royalist backers drafted the Argentine constitution, the provincial bosses, with the help of their gauchos, unseated him. Pueyrredón, in his effort to move toward centralized authority, had failed to reckon with his countrymen of the interior. These *caudillos* were the true lords of the countryside—each hating the other—but united by their common bond of hatred for the liberal *porteños*. By 1820, chaos had completely destroyed the creoles' vision of a modern nation (especially for those who had fought for Argentine independence) and had undone what little unity the United Provinces possessed. In this year alone, more than twenty governors ruled the province of Buenos Aires.

In September of 1820, General Martín Rodríguez was named provincial governor of Buenos Aires, a post he held until 1824. Rodríguez, though an able statesman, was overshadowed by his minister of government and foreign affairs, Bernardino Rivadavia. Rivadavia served in this post until 1824 when the governorship was shifted to Juan Gregorio de las Heras. The war with Brazil during the term of de las Heras persuaded the Buenos Aires leaders of the need for a strong government to deal with foreign trouble makers. In February 1826, they elected Bernardino Rivadavia president of the United Provinces. Rivadavia, however, was a *porteño,* a fact he never tried to hide; he never visited the interior and he had nothing but contempt for its *caudillos* and their gauchos. The hinterland *caudillos* in turn refused to accept his *porteño* leadership, and in 1827, faced with general revolt, Rivadavia resigned.

For two years the country was again faced with anarchy and civil war. The people demanded a strong leader—one who could quiet the storm of rebellion, and in 1829 they chose Juan Manuel de Rosas. Rosas, who ruled Argentina for 23 years, has been called "the caudillos' caudillo" and "the gauchos' gaucho." His term was known for its bloodshed and tyranny. Other powerful *caudillos* who opposed him were killed or driven into exile. Despite this bloody side of Rosas' dictatorship, a measure of stability and at least a semblance of national unity prevailed. Rosas was driven into exile in 1852 by a former ally, Justo José de Urquiza, who assumed power. Among the factors contributing to Rosas' overthrow was the growing appeal of the intellectual exiles who waged literary war against him, including Domingo Sarmiento, Esteban Echeverría, Juan Alberdi, and Bartolomé Mitre, and also the growing market for Argentine products in Europe.

CONSTITUTIONALISM

The political pattern for the next thirty years reflected government by an oligarchy of conservatives who functioned through a conservative political party that eventually assumed the name National Democratic Party. No opponents to the policies of the oligarchy were allowed to share in the government. Power was transmitted from one president to his selected successor in a closed caucus, and elections were controlled.

Within a year after taking office, Urquiza drafted the constitution under which Argentina is still governed and started the country on the road to an era of economic and political modernization. Between the years 1862 and 1874, two of her most dynamic sons ruled Argentina. Bartolomé Mitre was elected as the country's first constitutional president at a Congress in May 1862. Domingo Sarmiento succeeded him for the term 1868–1874. Both men were extremely patriotic and were pledged to the modernization of Argentina.

Provincial opposition to *porteño* domination of the presidency helped to bring about the election in 1874 of Nicolás Avellaneda, a native of Tucumán in the northern region of Argentina. Avellaneda continued to move in much the same direction as his two predecessors with respect to modernization. The centuries-long battle between Argentina and the Indians was ended during Avellaneda's administration which opened the way for the great surge into the rich pampas and for Argentina's unparalleled prosperity.

Under General Julio A. Roca, Avellaneda's successor, and his brother-in-law Juárez Celman, who succeeded him, the country's first true political parties were founded. Argentina's prosperity had fostered the growth of a large middle class and when the economic depression of the 1880's began to be felt, a group of political unknowns organized the Civic Union of Youth. The organization, agitating for free suffrage and honest elections, won wide public support. With Leandro Alem as president, the organization led a national revolt against Celman's administration. In April 1890, Celman's cabinet resigned en masse and in July Celman turned over the office to Vice President Carlos Pellegrini.

AN EXPERIMENT IN DEMOCRACY

The 1890 uprising did not eradicate the oligarchy of landlords and merchants but it did mark the beginning of a political battle between the old regime and the "Radicals" as the Civic Union of Youth came to be called. The old oligarchy ruled until 1916 when the Radicals finally came to power. Roque Saenz Peña, president from 1910 to 1916, led the way for the Radicals' victory. Saenz Peña promised honest elections, effective suffrage, and the participation of all political sectors in the Government. In 1912 he pushed through Congress his electoral reform law (the Saenz Peña law): a reform that would make democracy effective and would promote the two-party system. The result was the first really free election in modern Argentina and the election of the first Radical Party candidate, Hipólito Irigoyen. Irigoyen was succeeded by Marcelo de Alvear in 1922 but was re-elected for a second term in 1928.

Irigoyen and his successor Marcelo de Alvear had a perfect opportunity to return the Government to democracy; instead, they did very little to reduce the influence of the landholders and continued the policy of centralization in the Government. For the fourteen years the Radical Party ruled (1916–1930), little hope for democracy could be seen. Irigoyen in his two terms intervened more frequently in the provinces than had any other Argentine president. His tendency to use the Radical Party as a vehicle for his personal gain finally led to a split in the Party during Alvear's administration. In 1928, Irigoyen was asked to run for re-election. He was elected almost effortlessly, but the country's high expectations were again smashed—not only because of Irigoyen's ineptitude but also because of the world depression which would have made problems for any administration. It was these two factors together—the world depression and his inability to counter its disastrous effects in Argentina—that dealt the final blow to his regime. Thus, on September 6, 1930, an army unit entered Buenos Aires to depose Irigoyen and met little resistance, marking the end of an era of abstinence from military intervention in national and local politics.

THE RETURN OF TOTALITARIANISM

General José Uriburu assumed control with a dictatorship unlike anything Argentina had experienced since Rosas. President Uriburu's attempt to impose a Fascist system with an elite minority in control was unsuccessful however, and he finally agreed to hold elections in 1931. The Conservatives, joined by some Radicals, elected Agustín Justo and returned Argentina to the pre-1914 oligarchy system.

At the outbreak of World War II in 1939, President Roberto Ortiz, Justo's successor, proclaimed Argentina neutral. He was however in open sympathy with the Allies which tended to alienate the Axis sympathizers. A diabetic and almost totally blind, Ortiz was compelled to vacate the presidency in mid-1940 because of his illness, and his vice-president, Ramón Castillo, became acting president. Castillo's "neutrality" was pro-Axis. He suppressed any popular sympathy for the Allies and allowed the pro-Axis press to run. Castillo was fast becoming one of Argentina's more unpopular presidents. His pro-Axis attitude made him anathema to the liberals; the oligarchs resented his intention to impose his own choice as successor in the September 1943 elections; and the wage earners were feeling the pinch of the high cost of living at a time when the nation was supposedly prospering. When Castillo announced his choice for president, Robustiano Costas, a wealthy landholder in the northern province of Salta, the pro-Axis military faction joined the pro-Allied group and in June 1943 overthrew the government in a *coup d'état*. The junta which took over the reins of government was composed of a group of military officers called the *Grupo de oficiales unidos* (the G.O.U.)—all scrambling for power. The struggle culminated in 1946 with the coming to power of Juan Perón.

THE PERONIST PHASE AND ITS AFTERMATH

It is difficult to consider all the ramifications of Perón's regime in a few lines or pages. Perhaps it can best be explained as an authoritarian-democracy or as an exemplar of contemporary *caudillismo* in action. Because of his near overthrow by the liberals in 1945 and the narrowness of his plurality in the February 1946 elections, he was obliged to hide his objectives behind a cloak of representative government. Perón's tool to gain control over the country was his skillful use of persuasion rather than force. Universities were purged and government-appointed *interventores* were placed in control of them. The Supreme Court was also purged by Perón's subordinates in Congress. Critics of the regime, such as opposition parties and the press, were brought under control by such methods as cutting off newspaper supplies or imposition of fines. Thus, Perón was able to cast a cloak of legitimacy over his true objectives of establishing an industrialized, nationalistic state in which a controlled labor force would be part of a controlled economy under a military government.

Perón's re-election in 1951 in one of the country's most corrupt elections proved beyond any question that this was not a democratic regime; the following year his wife Evita (his right arm and vice-president) died of cancer. Perón tried desperately to hold his totalitarian government together, and whenever his position was threatened he would apply his divide-and-conquer tactics to his own followers as well as to the opposition. By 1954 he had alienated the Church, a staunch backer in the earlier elections, and had deepened the hostility between the working class and the upper class. In September 1955, after several months of planning, the military—including the army under General Eduardo Lonardi and the navy under Admiral Isaac Rojas, ousted Perón.

General Lonardi, who headed the government as provisional president, was removed from office after only eight weeks by his fellow officers. A five-man junta took control until the restoration of civilian control on May 1, 1958. The junta, headed by General Pedro Aramburu, reinstated the original 1853 Argentine constitution, and in February 1958 held free national elections.

Dr. Arturo Frondizi, the candidate of the Intransigent Radical Party (*Unión Cívica-Radical Intransigente*) was elected by 45 per cent of the popular vote. Before the administration was eight months old, however, Frondizi had alienated his own supporters, and by November had to suspend constitutional rights and use the state of siege which he maintained almost constantly until his overthrow in 1962. Yet his greatest foe was the military —which had seen to it that free elections were held in 1958. The military however, was bitterly divided regarding the problems and solutions facing the country. In 1962, Frondizi decided to let the Peronists run their own candidates (but they could not use the party label of *Peronista*) in the gubernatorial and congressional elections. The Peronists, using the label *Justicialista,* won ten governorships including Buenos Aires and a substantial minority of the 46 seats in the Chamber of Deputies. The military immediately demanded that the President annul the elections—which he agreed to do in part. He agreed to annul five of the provincial elections in which the Peronists had won without the aid of other parties. This was not enough for the army and on March 30, 1962, Frondizi was removed from office and exiled to the Island of Martín García.

Senate President José María Guido was sworn in as President and the 1962 elections were annulled. After a year of violent political crises and conflicts which verged on civil war, national elections were held and constitutional government restored. An indication of the many conflicts apparent in Argentina is the fact that the new president, Arturo Illia, won only 26 per cent of the popular vote, and that 24 different parties won seats in the national congress.

After Illia's election, the country seemed to pause for a sigh of relief. The Argentines, even those who had not voted for Illia, were apparently ready to get the country moving forward again. Their optimism was short lived, however. During the next three years, the country was faced with heavy unemployment, inflation, labor strikes, and a foreign debt of catastrophic proportions. The *Peronistas,* badly split in 1963, had sufficiently united by 1965 to cause many obstacles for Illia, and in the Congressional elections held that year won 36 per cent of the vote. Unable to cope with the Peronists and inflation, Arturo Illia was ousted in June, 1966, and Lieutenant General Juan Carlos Onganía installed as president. One of the first acts of Onganía's government was to dissolve political parties in order to "bring about the rapid achievement of national unity and modernization for the country."

THE IMPORT OF POLITICAL STABILITY/ INSTABILITY: AN ASSESSMENT

Perhaps this pattern of atomization and instability which we have brought to light in this brief political account can be explained as a consequence of the post-independence decision taken by Argentina, as well as the other new Latin American states, to organize its political institutions according to foreign models, which, later were found to be incompatible with its traditional ideas and rising expectations.[2]

The idea of concensus based on stable government through elite unity seems not to have taken as much root in the present stage of Argentine development as has the idea of charismatic leadership. The latter, whether in the form of an open or disguised dictatorship, seems far more attractive than the prospect of an impersonal, democratic arrangement of political authority. For the policy-making structures, the problems of stimulating development have been confronted either through mobilization systems of coercion or through permissive strategies of social change. Both methods have achieved varying degrees of success in the evolution of Argentine modernization. The latter, it might be said, closely relates to the *belle époque* of stability characterizing the period 1862 through 1930 during which the Argentine nation made significant economic, demographic, and cultural gains. On the other hand, coercive mobilization distinguished itself first during the Rosas period which saw the forcible unification of the national territory, and later on in the Peronist era during which another form of synthetic national integration took place.

It would seem, then, that indecision regarding choice of a strategy for development rather than national circumstance has contributed to a situation of endemic instability in Argentina. As compared with the other developing nations of Latin America, Asia, and Africa, the Argentine context has been ideal for successful realization of efforts toward development when one considers the favorable attributes of climate, demography, social homogeneity, and an abundant expertise in its labor force. Nevertheless, different interpretations of the national interest have tended to cripple efforts on the part of the modernizing elites toward the clarification of political means to obtain national objectives. It has been difficult to construct a single network of authority to propel and regulate change in the political system.

It can be argued that Argentine nationalism has tended to retard rather than encourage the process of developing political structures capable of converting demands of modernization into workable policy. This facet of development is particularly pointed up in the recruitment process which has tended to discourage a participant citizenry while at the same time engendering an incohesive form of leadership.

Alluding to the relationship between political development and leadership, the Argentine writer Félix Luna points out that Argentina has never lacked leadership to promote its national goals of development; yet, it has invariably been the fate of this leadership to suffer rejection either through *coup d'état* or forced exile in the process of mobilizing national awareness for the realization of development goals.[3] Dr. Arturo Illia has been the most recent casualty in the Argentine struggle for political development. Like his predecssor, Dr. Arturo Frondizi, Illia strove to awaken national interest in a *plan de desarrollo* by deliberate efforts to bring into the stream of decision-making the opinions of all sectors in the Argentine polity. This basic aspiration was clearly worded in his last presidential message:

> "Political parties, labor organizations, business groups, universities and all representative institutions of the nation are formally required to seek out together with the Executive the best way to unite the Argentine people with a conscience capable of consolidating our greatness." [4]

To date, no prescription has been formulated for the malady besetting Argentine leadership, because in reality the phenomenon has been too diffuse for accurate study. There is no monolithic structure of elitist power providing a solidary model of decision-making in the political process; rather leadership falls somewhere in the elitist-pluralist continuum. Political group involvement in any aggregable form is sporadic once the attainment of political influence is achieved.

In order to legitimize a political system, be it fascism or democracy, the maximum convergence of attitudes in support of that system is indispensable. Argentina has not shown any predilection for any one specific form of government. One might say it is now in quest of some system to regulate the competition which is inevitable in its diffuse power structure and to determine at the same time a mechanism for choosing those who lead.

NOTES

1. For a general description of political life and leadership in Argentina, the author has gleaned valuable material from numerous scholarly sources. The following might be of special interest to the reader: Barager, ed., *Why Perón Came to Power;* McGann, *Argentina: The Divided Land;* Rennie, *The Argentine Republic;* Romero, *A History of Argentine Political Thought;* Whitaker, *Argentina.*

2. Cf. Grondona, "Golpe o Legalidad?" p. 20.

3. Luna, *La Historia Argentina en Función de los Objetivos Nacionales,* pp. 13–14.

4. Illia, "Mensaje Presidencial," *Diario de Sesiones Cámara de Senadores de la Nación,* May 1, 1966, p. 19. (Author's translation.)

CHAPTER 3

THE ROLE OF GROUPS
IN THE POLITICAL
SOCIALIZATION PROCESS

THE POWER STRUCTURE AND THE
LEGITIMACY PROBLEM

The Argentine power structure is composed of various competing groups. These groups may be considered as the power elite, comprising principally military, labor, church, business, education, party, and government subsystems. Together with other social and political structures—family, school, bureaucracy, and electoral system—these subsystems share in the general political recruitment and socialization function. Furthermore, they are responsible for producing in the citizenry the basic attitudes required for legitimizing the political system.[1]

This is no easy task. To date, it has been relatively impossible to instill in the Argentine people any substantial degree of loyalty toward the numerous governments which have played a role in the political life of the country. The propriety of the political norms established by various governments has invariably been questioned, which has only served to make the maintenance of political systems short-lived.

In the Argentine political system, the political culture gives the appearance of being largely fragmented and heterogeneous in character. This has greatly restricted the effectiveness of parliamentary politics in Argentina, crippled the decision-making function of constitutionally elected regimes, and engendered military coups in the country. What is suggested here is that deliberate processes of political socialization, whether based on the philosophical rationale of emancipation, integration, popular sovereignty, social justice, or economic development, have failed to create a continuing sense of legitimacy in the political process. It has been increasingly difficult for the political system to adjust to disruptive changes inevitable as the society experiences various stages of transition to modernity.[2]

ALIENATION: STUMBLING BLOCK TO LEGITIMACY

It is difficult to detect on the part of the average Argentine any marked sense of belonging to the political system as such; his affective ties seem to be linked more to an ideal fraught with nationalism, lacking the substance of organized political action.[3] Simply, the predicament of the Argentine man-in-the-street is disorientation and his need is for political points of reference to provide him with direction and protection.[4]

Through empirical study, the Argentine sociologist, José Enrique Miguens, has been able to ascertain some characteristics of the mass man present in all strata of Argentine society. The modal attitudes discovered reflect a general pattern of anomie, frustration, aggression, and over-all negative disposition to the political process and involvement therein. In his analysis of the problem, Miguens indicated that prestige of the police, labor, parliamentary, and political leadership was at an all-time low; a general air of crisis in confidence toward society prevailed, concomitant with varying incidence of social prejudice directed against such standard national scapegoats as the military, foreign capitalism, communism, and politicians.[5] From the standpoint of social composition and political leadership, the Miguens analysis also revealed that all these isolative attitudes predominated in the university-educated, upper-class sectors, and a large segment of the population of greater Buenos Aires favored a dictatorial regime for problem-solving purposes.[6] These data provide us with a rough approximation of the effects of acculturation in Argentina.

The immigration deluge of the 1930's and the attending impact of industrialization and urbanization in the port area also caused problems for integration of the citizenry into the polity. It could even be argued that the immigration offspring, the middle class, still remains diffident regarding its capacity to influence political decisions in the polity.[7]

The general decline of the arrangement of traditional *caudillismo,* which provided a haven for the middle class, exacerbated the political atomization of this sector, driving it into the arms of the labor syndicates. The middle class had found refuge in Perón, the *caudillo máximo* of the middle- and lower-class elements. It took the *Revolución Libertadora,* which toppled Perón eventually, to restore to the people the liberty of deciding in free elections. However, from a state of political passivism under Perón the people were thrust into a state of political activism. They were asked to think for themselves, to make responsible decisions, to exercise individualism at the polls. The responsibilities inherent in the setting up of a democratic, constitutional process were too onerous and merely intensified rather than allayed the fears and insecurities of the Argentine people.

In the Peronist wake, President Aramburu inherited a people whose minds had been liberated by the revolution of 1955, who were given an opportunity to think and decide for themselves for the first time in more than a decade. It is important to keep this point in mind as we appraise the tumultuous state and disorganization in which the political system finds itself even at the present.

The general consensus is that, out of the disorder and disorientation which the Argentine people are now experiencing, progress will be made toward a viable political development, but the great virtue of patience, both on the part of some sectors in the Argentine political community and on the part of others abroad (the United States included), is desperately needed and must be exercised. Within this framework, the 1966 revolution against constitutional President Illia may have retarded the process of political socialization aimed at stimulating a close participation of all sectors in the Argentine system.

Despite the impressive benefits derived from past economic and social development, Argentina has tended to fall short of cultural fusion in the sense that the gap between the interests of agrarian and industrial sectors has been difficult to bridge.[8]

In terms of Argentine nation-building, the most important question is whether or not the processes of socialization can provide a political elite which will value modernization above all else. It is reasonable to assume that salient political groups operating in the polity represent a modernizing leadership which, appropriately enough, is pointed up in the nationalism which pervades varied spheres of political activity. As the common denominator of all political and socializing functions in the Argentine system, this nationalism gears itself to a nation-building function manifested by the interests of different groups generally bent on upholding national dignity and maintenance of the nation state. These groups, as discussed below, inject into the political sector through their respective ideologies of leadership certain norms or dominant modes of orientation to political life.

THE CHURCH

Recognition of the church in its fundamental theological position vis-à-vis the state would seem to preclude direct involvement in the politicization function. Still, the Argentine experience has revealed the reputation of this ecclesiastical organization to provide political direction wherever the interests of religion or Catholic nationalism are involved.[9] As the spiritual beacon of a predominantly Catholic community legitimized by the Constitution, the Argentine church has duly carried out its moral indoctrination activities with close regard for its inherent political responsibility.

Politically, the modernizing spirit which characterized this Catholic nationalism found expression in the democratizing role the church assumed in Argentine politics. The traditional, antiliberal Catholic nationalism of the 1870's gave way to a more secularized nationalist orientation geared to the actualization of political liberties.[10] With this focus the church is now striving to shape political attitudes to a democratic political culture.

THE UNIVERSITY

Another important structure conditioning the modernizing milieu in Argentina is the political university.[11] The political attitudes generated by the university community, taken collectively, represent the expanding need of intellectual leadership to cope with an all-pervading national problem: modernization.

Political mobilization in the direction of national development goals forms one of the basic ideological strands governing the university political-orientation structure. To this end, the Argentine universities have been moving, stimulating through their reformist ideas concern for social change and economic development. The all-important concern in this regard has been the preservation of university autonomy from political intervention in order that the university and political community may be duly served. So far, however, university nationalism in Argentina, as manifested in development attitudes toward nation-building problems, has not been able to bridge the gap between traditional and modern elements in the polity.

It would be equivocal to define the political influence ascribed to the Argentine university structure merely in terms of its nationalistic, ideological function in the political environment. Without discounting the significance of the latter, consideration should also be given to the importance of the university's role as an agency for the training of Argentine leadership. An examination of leadership composition in Argentina for example, would reveal a significant percentage of university graduates occupying political elite posts.[12]

Depending on the level of participation and involvement in politics as an ideology articulator, the university may generate or destroy orientations of support toward the political regime in the future holders of political power. This is a constant reality with which political leaders in Argentina and elsewhere have had to live. It is not surprising that Perón in his Justicialist Constitution of 1949 enlisted the strategic services of the universities to mold a political leadership to a specific national culture.[13] Nor is it surprising that General Onganía resorted to political intervention to mobilize support for the necessary national "recuperation" envisioned by his Argentine revolution.[14] In a modernizing context such as that of Argentina, the political orientation role of the university cannot be side-stepped nor encroached upon without serious side effects for the nation-building process.

THE BUSINESS SECTOR

Another dynamic group which is increasing its sphere of influence in the political ideological life of the country is the *empresario* or business sector. Traditionally, the principal national activity of this group has been concentrated in the economy, leaving the affairs of the polity to the more articulate military, labor, and university groups. To understand the withdrawal from politics of the *empresario* sector, one must examine the social dynamics of Argentine political development.

Briefly, it can be noted that with the coming of Perón the traditional upper class withdrew from the political scene to the confines of the *estancia,* remaining for the most part aloof from politics in general. Furthermore, the great immigration (or *aluvión)* which deluged Argentina caused great insecurity among the children of immigrants concerned with social mobility. These immigrants formed the core of the *empresario* sector; but, to the degree that they withdrew from the responsibilities of assuming public office, they weakened the group and thus inhibited its role in the political process.

In appraising the traditionally low level of political participation in the *empresario* sector, it is also necessary to take into
account the economic motivation of this group—making money
and the acquisition of wealth and prestige through channels
other than those which would entail the responsibilities of public
or political office. The *empresario* segment is considered an efficient class, but—unlike, for example, the labor syndicate—weak
as a political group. One may hypothesize that inasmuch as the
industrialization process is still new in Argentina, the *empresarios* do not feel they can spare the time from their business
endeavors to devote to politics.

In discussing the business sector one should distinguish the
agropecuario class, that is the big farmers and ranchers, from
the *empresario* or business sector. The former tends to be more
independent and secure from the standpoint of status in the
society. On balance, however, it cannot be denied that both
empresarios and *agropecuarios* are becoming increasingly articulate politically.

As mentioned earlier, the *empresario* group is just beginning
to define itself in the political sphere. As a result it is not easy
to make any definitive generalizations about its political values
and ideology in the political system. Its behavior in the present
stage of development reveals a modernizing nationalism with
strong democratic overtones.[15] No matter what ideological framework is adopted, it can be safely assumed that the role of the
empresario sector will be an energetic and progressive one.

THE MILITARY

An important sector which gravitates considerably more than
business into the political system is the military. Like the business
sector, the military possesses a wide range of *técnicos* or men of
expertise fully capable of dealing with the problem of development in Argentina. Prior to the 1966 coup, a national senator
insisted to the writer that the military is far more professionalized [16] than it was at the time the Frondizi administration was
overthrown. He stressed that the military was well-read, politically

informed, and perhaps politically capable of assuming the reins of government and managing them satisfactorily.

Examined as one of the major systems of political socialization in Argentina, the military operates as an institutional interest group which carries out social and political functions besides the articulation of interests in the political system.[17] Bearing this in mind, it may be useful to appraise the involvement of this sector from the standpoint of its over-all negative or positive contribution to the Argentine system.

Whenever the military has intervened in the political arena there appears to have been a strong incidence of political tension and social anxiety throughout the civilian sector of the country.[18] It can be generally assumed that military involvement in Argentine politics has been a product, if not a concomitant factor, of severe tensions relating to the cultural, political, and social spheres of the country. The political socialization function of the military may be characterized in terms of its over-all goal to maintain stability in a tension-free political environment—preferably through national institutions, or, if the situation warrants it, through revolution of the *Cuartelazo, Machetismo, Golpe de Estado,* or Palace type.

Viewing the matter in this light perhaps helps to explain the profound military involvement which has characterized Argentine politics over the past three decades. Since 1930, the military as an interest structure has found it necessary to intervene in the government of Argentina through revolutionary action five times. Beginning in 1930, the government of Hipólito Irigoyen was overthrown by General Uriburu; in 1943 General Ramírez toppled the government of Ramón Castillo which culminated in the coming to power of Juan Perón in 1946; in 1955, a coalition of officers ousted the government of Perón; in March 1962 a successful coup was staged against the first constitutionally elected president following Perón, Arturo Frondizi; and in June 1966, Arturo Illia was removed from office.

San Martín is often quoted as saying: "The army is a lion that must be kept in a cage and not let out until the day of battle." This political attitude no longer holds true; the military in Argentina has become increasingly politicized, as its participation in the revolutionary activities of the past three decades has clearly shown. The political orientations of the military indeed reflect an ambiguous brand of constitutionalism, stemming from the dilemma of how to comply with the Constitution and have a representative form of government if, in effect, free elections mean a strong possibility of a return to power of the Peronists. The basic rationale of this precarious constitutionalism is a pretorian nationalism of which as Fitzgibbon puts it, "[the] Armies sometimes become the self-appointed custodians. . . ." [19]

Inherent in the political behavior of the military is a modernizing nationalism which has influenced the whole idea of *golpismo* or military intervention in the political system. This modernizing nationalism cannot be understood unless certain basic characteristics about the military in Argentina are understood. It should be noted, for example, that the Argentine military is prochurch, pronationalism and traditions, is anticommunist in orientation, pro-social-order, but also revolutionary. The general observation is that the military is development-oriented—wanting country and government to develop faster so that the nation will no longer have need of foreign investment which is considered a threat to national sovereignty.

Equally important is the professional spirit developed by the military considering the abundance of expertise to be found within its ranks. Military impatience with the workings of such democratic mechanisms as the party system should also be taken into account. It would be an overstatement to argue that the military is trigger-happy where revolutionary measures are concerned. That they are in a hurry to realize the goals of modernization perhaps best describes their revolutionary anxiety.

The basic tenets of this modernizing nationalism in the military sector were clearly spelled out in the Message to the Argentine People by the Revolutionary Junta which installed General Onganía as President. This message states in part, that

The modernizing of the country cannot be delayed and constitutes a challenge to the imagination, energy and pride of Argentines.

Change and modernization are the concrete terms of a

formula of well-being which recognizes, as a basic and primary assumption, the unity of Argentines.

For it [modernization], it was indispensable to eliminate the fallacy of a formal and sterile legality beneath whose protection was carried out a policy of division and opposition which made unreal the possibility of combined effort and rejected authority so that the armed forces . . . comes to fill the vacuum of such authority and leadership before Argentine dignity fades forever.[20]

THE LABOR SECTOR

Sometimes complementary and sometimes antagonistic to the orientations of the military sector is the political role of labor in Argentina. The political influence of labor is intimately related to the entire process of modernization which has taken place in the country. With the growth of larger urban industrial centers, labor syndicates emerged and broke the monopoly of power once held by the traditional *caudillos* over the masses. It should be pointed out that traditional *caudillismo* in Argentina, as it was known prior to the coming of urbanization, is just about passé.

It is generally agreed that there is no danger that the labor movement, as represented by its leading exponent, the CGT (*Confederación General de Trabajadores*), will lose its hold as an important factor of power in the Argentine system. Especially in official circles, it is felt it would be better for the labor movement to discard political ideology and function on a more pragmatic basis to resolve the political issues of the time. The argument is that if labor could forget ideology, workable competition between labor and business could be achieved, thus paving the road to development. It is becoming more evident that labor and government leaders are striving to agree upon some common approach to speed up the development of the country. The military also seems to be trying to "mix" more with the labor (Peronist) sector, as though wanting to establish more rapport with deference to its (Peronist) ideological base.

As the mother organization of all labor, the CGT is in a strategic position to mold the political attitudes of a large segment of the Argentine people. It is well known that its leadership ideology is in no way whatsoever apolitical. It is true that in the Perón era the Confederation did participate more overtly in the political process, but with time and the application of the Law of Professional Associations it has for legal purposes had to remain on the fringe of politics.

Notwithstanding its anticommunist orientation, the CGT admits there are communist unions in its fold. These unions are proportionately small and profess a political unionism of the Moscow-Peking variety, which seeks to take advantage of the entire labor movement. Collectively, the communist unions are known under the general label of MUCS (*Movimiento de Unidad y Coordinación Sindical*). The reason why the MUCS adheres to the CGT, a labor leader remarked, is because the communists traditionally tend to rally to those groups which represent the masses. The CGT is such an organization. 'The labor leader pointed out that the MUCS *buscan carne de cultivo* literally, "seeks meat on which to grow," in an organization such as the CGT. The general observation is that the MUCS, though still in the minority, possesses a superior organizational structure to that of the CGT and this is where the threat, if any, exists that the communists may completely take over such a powerful labor organization.

The organizational superiority of the MUCS is attributed to the efficiency displayed in their activity of political socialization, demonstrated especially in the manner in which they carry out their proselyting. It is known that the MUCS has schools in which it indoctrinates and turns out staunch militants. It is also known that the CGT has similar schools, but, the Peronist sector argues, the schools of the MUCS have no financial problems whatsoever since they are supported from outside. It can be hypothesized, then, that to the extent that the CGT is not dominated by the communists, it can serve as a barrier to communist success among the masses depending on whether or not it can run its schools as efficiently as the MUCS does.

Basically, the educational program of the CGT consists in courses to train leadership. These *Cursos Gremiales,* as they are called, cover a wide range of topics in the fields of economics, politics, law, etc., and are taught by eminent professors of different political ideologies. This program cannot be taken lightly, since it is from this source that the new leaders emerge who will be in charge of running the unions throughout the country.

It is known that many of the leaders who have graduated from the *Cursos Gremiales* have either abandoned labor or moved up the labor ranks to assume important political posts. This is the upcoming thing in political leadership—the birth of the *políticos gremiales.* This is the new group that, as the Argentines say, *hace cola,* or is influential, and has a promising future in the political elite. Those who aspire to political power are finding the unions and the political unionism they represent a splendid avenue into the circle of the elect. Those who aspire to political office work through the unions to realize their political ambitions because in the traditional *caudillo* arrangement they have less chance of doing this, simply because the little *caudillos* take all the important posts. One might say the unions afford the prospective political aspirant a greater margin to work out his political ambitions.

The increasing importance ascribed to labor in the process of political development is assessed with cautious optimism. Former president Illia, for example, made it clear that "unions are useful and necessary institutions in contemporary life; . . . but union activity cannot nor should transform itself into partisan political activity. . . ." [21] There is little debate regarding the Peronist, partisan character of the labor structure in Argentina. Yet, as Dardo Cúneo argues, this phenomenon should be understood in terms of the very diversity of *peronismo* which has a "political" as well as a "syndicalist" base; the former stands for the past, the latter for the present.[22] It would seem difficult for the Peronist past and the Peronist present to coexist harmoniously under the same labor roof; the new will either give way to the old or vice versa. The outcome will undoubtedly influence the political ideas and demands which labor will inject into the political system.

THE POLITICAL EXECUTIVE

In the interest of the polity, the political executive, sometimes referred to as the *poder ejecutivo, gobierno,* or *presidente,* assumes the responsibility of regulating the over-all process of political socialization as performed by such groups as the church, business, university, military, labor, and other agencies in the political system. This enormous responsibility is backed up by the awesome power consigned to Argentine Executives in Article 86 of the National Constitution of 1853. What the Constitution did in effect was to institutionalize a system of *presidentes fuertes,* that is, strong presidents with practically omnipotent authority.[23]

The political executive in Argentina is constitutionally "the supreme head of the Nation and in charge of the general administration of the country." [24] He has a carte blanche to political power which can make him totalitarian or democrat. The executive may exercise this political power to protect and to promote programs of national growth. The degree of involvement in national programs vary, of course, with the diversity of Argentine executive leadership. For Argentine leaders like Mario Moreno, Bernardino Rivadavia, and Juan Manuel de Rosas, the exercise of executive power concerned the problem of Argentine integration or disintegration; for Mitre and Sarmiento, the major preoccupation was in a program of economic progress for the country; for Irigoyen the national goal was democratization; for Perón, his leadership appeared as a myopic scheme for social justice; for Frondizi and Illia, the plan was for the establishment of a cohesive political community; and recently for Onganía the plan appears to be a concern with national security.

It should be emphasized that the paramount goal of the executive power structure in Argentina is national consensus and legitimacy. There is no realistic way of achieving this goal except by inducing the support of the variegated groups which provide political orientation and guidance in the body politic. In essence such an approach would require a willingness on the part of interest groups to discard political ideology in favor of a workable methodology for development. This is indeed a large order, given the diversity of the Argentine political system.

As indicated in Chapter II, the political record in Argentina reveals a variety of executive styles in coping with the problem of national consensus and legitimacy. Frondizi, for example, considered it imperative to include in his government all shades of public opinion notwithstanding political ideology. In his *Mensaje de Pacificación y Desarrollo Nacional,* Frondizi spelled out that the political executive should govern for all Argentines regardless of political affiliation; that he should strive for the support of all interest groups, "promoting meetings and consultations with political parties, with union leaders . . . with men of science, with technicians and professionals, with regional representative institutions. . . ." [25] In effect Frondizi singled out the point that development could not proceed in Argentina until all sectors were given a representative voice in the government. Illia also recognized the importance of this concept of "confraternity." He appealed to all political sectors to harmonize their differences with a spirit of compromise; and implored their political participation, promising that "no hypothesis would be rejected without examination." [26] As the record shows, it was difficult to aggregate interests on this simple basis of political realism.

Where two constitutional political executives failed, the president of a revolutionary government has tried to succeed. The problem of directing the forces of socialization in Argentina is for General Onganía and his regime to resolve. Simply stated, he seeks "to promote a greater participation by the citizenry in the orientation and manifestation of the political life of the country. . . ." [27] To accomplish this goal he proposes to use "basic organizations" throughout the community to produce what he calls "the political man." In this regard, "all extremisms" are condemned, as well as "third positions or material or opportunistic eclecticisms." [28]

It must be noted that Onganía finds himself in a political cul-de-sac. There is little support for his revolutionary policies within the various sectors discussed above. The church seems to be exercising an attitude of neutrality rather than sympathy for the present regime. Student movements have generally militated against Onganía's policies of intervention in the university, but by themselves do not appear to be a significant threat to the administration. The business sector finds it advantageous to remain aloof from Onganía's revolutionary policies. The military, which put Onganía into power, does not manifest complete support for his government because of what is viewed as *status quo* politics. Labor, backed up by the Peronists, appears to be the greatest threat to Onganía; they are aware of the political vacuum that exists in the country and are prepared to take advantage of this situation by organizing a populist movement with the help of the armed forces.

It appears that Onganía is left very little alternative but to revert to constitutional mechanisms of party activity and elections in the very near future.

NOTES

1. David Apter provides some valuable insights on the problem of legitimacy. He states, for example, that "a particular form of government is institutionalized only when it becomes morally valid. Hence, legitimacy is related to a set of conceptions held by significant members of the polity about the rightness of a political pattern, which, in turn, provides the pattern with a set of proprieties." *The Politics of Modernization*, p. 236. See also Lipset, *Political Man*, Chapter III.

2. See David Easton's reference to "politicization" and its relation to legitimacy in "An Approach to the Analysis of Political Systems," pp. 383–400.

3. Cf. Fernández, "The Nationalism Syndrome in Argentina," *passim*.

4. This existentialist motif is expressed in the writings of several Argentine writers. See Mafud, *Psicología de la Viveza Criolla;* Ortiz, *El Hombre que está solo y espera;* Sebreli, *Buenos Aires Vida Cotidiana y Alienación*.

5. Miguens, "Un Análisis del Fenómemo," in *Argentina 1930–1960*, pp. 348–349.

6. *Ibid.*, p. 349.

7. For an excellent discussion of the immigration and urbanization problem, see Whitaker, *Argentina*, pp. 53–59; also see Beyhaut, *et al.*, "Los Inmigrantes en el Sistema Occupacional Argentina," in *Argentina, Sociedad de Masas*, p. 119.

8. For an interesting discussion of the concepts of cultural fusion and acculturation, together with other closely connected terms relating to most theories of social change, see Ponsioen, *The Analysis of Social Change Reconsidered*, pp. 50–56.

9. See Kennedy, *Catholicism, Nationalism, and Democracy in Argentina, passim*.

10. Adúriz, "Religión," in *Argentina 1930–1960*, p. 424.

11. Harrison, "The Confrontation with the Political University," pp. 74–83.

12. Silvert, *The Conflict Society*, p. 120. Table III in this book substantiates Professor Silvert's findings.

13. *Constitución Justicialista*, Article 37, paragraph 4.

14. News items in *La Nación*, August 1, 1966, and August 8, 1966.

15. See excerpts of speech delivered by the President of Unión Industrial Argentina in *La Nación*, May 16, 1966. See also text of speech delivered by the President of Sociedad Rural Argentina in *La Nación*, August 1, 1966; also *La Nación*, June 6, 1966, for speech delivered by President of ACIEL and editorial in *La Nación*, June 27, 1966.

16. That is, "professionalized" to function as a modernizing force and not simply as an institution for "preserving internal order and defending the nation against external threats." In this view, political involvement of the military is rationalized, even if not justified; see Lieuwen, *Arms and Politics in Latin America*, p. 34. See also Orsolini, *Ejército Argentino y Crecimiento Nacional, passim*. On the possible constructive role of the military in the new states, see Johnson, *The Military and Society in Latin America, passim*.

17. Almond's Introduction to Almond and Coleman, eds., *The Politics of the Developing Areas*, pp. 33–34.

18. Sueldo, "Fuerzas Armadas," in *Argentina 1930–1960*, pp. 159–177.

19. Fitzgibbon, "What Price Latin American Armies," pp. 521–522.

20. *Boletín Oficial de la República Argentina* (Buenos Aires: Dirección Nacional del Registro Oficial, July 8, 1966), pp. 1–2. (Author's translation.)

21. News item in *La Nación,* May 2, 1966. (Author's translation.)

22. Cúneo, *Informes,* pp. 78–79.

23. Levene *et al., Presidentes Argentinos,* pp. 7–9; see also Viamonte, *Manual de Derecho Constitucional,* Chapters XLIV and LVII.

24. *Argentine Constitution,* Article 86. (Author's translation.)

25. Frondizi, *Mensaje de Pacificación y Desarrollo Nacional* (Read before the Legislative Assembly by the President of the Nation, Dr. Arturo Frondizi, on the inauguration of this constitutional period), pp. 14–15. (Author's translation.)

26. Illia, "Mensaje Presidencial," *Diario de Sesiones Cámara de Senadores de la Nación,* May 1, 1966. (Author's translation.)

27. News item in *La Nación,* August 8, 1966. (Author's translation.)

28. *Ibid.*

CHAPTER 4

THE PARTY FUNCTION
IN THE RECRUITMENT PROCESS

The political system, as mentioned earlier, has, through its group structures, the responsibility of political recruitment and socialization. In periods of constitutional stability, this important function has largely been performed in Argentina by means of the political party system.

As one of the most important agencies of political socialization, a great deal is expected of the party system as demands for higher status and achievement increase in the modernizing society. One might speculate that awareness of party omnipotence vis-à-vis other interest groups in the system would tend psychologically to destroy any confidence on the part of the citizenry in regard to the modernization potential and workability of this democratic institution.

POLITICAL PARTY LEGITIMACY

The Argentine scholar Germán Bidart Campos describes the Argentine political party as one of the main "unofficial" pro-

39

tagonists in the political system ("unofficial" in the sense that political parties are not embodied in the formal text of the constitutional system, notwithstanding the freedom of association clause contained in Article 14 and the unenumerated constitutional guarantees in Article 33).[1] According to César Romero, political parties were purposely ignored in the Constitution of 1853 because they were considered "contrary to the interests of the nation."[2] Romero points out however that the silence of the Constitution should not be interpreted to mean the "exclusion" or "prohibition" of political parties from the Argentine system.[3] Underlying severe criticisms of the function of parties in Argentina is a general consensus as to the strategically critical role which party structures could play in the process of coordinating and balancing demands of all major interests in the Argentine nation.[4] The modernizing elites are fully aware that Argentine modernization in the direction of democracy is hardly possible without the active cooperation of political parties. Thus, there is widespread interest in legitimizing the status of political parties even if it requires reforming the supreme law of the land.[5]

It should be mentioned that in the more modern provincial constitutions, such as those of the provinces of Entre Ríos, Chaco, Chubut, Neuquén, and Río Negro, there are specific clauses legitimizing the existence of political parties.[6] In an effort to clear up the constitutional ambiguity surrounding the function of parties in the political system, Argentine constitutionalists offer the argument that political parties are implicitly recognized in the national Constitution, their reasoning being that the two concepts, political parties and democracy, are inseparable, one cannot exist without the other.[7] Argentine political elites are aware of this. They know that in a nation such as Argentina which is committed to the process of democratic constitutionalism, the *appearance* of democracy is not enough; without the *essence* —namely, political parties—the goal of representative government is practically unobtainable. These are the hard facts of a politics of democracy which now more than ever are carefully being debated in civilian as well as official circles.

THE FUNCTIONAL UTILITY OF PARTIES

Criticisms are leveled however, against the prerevolutionary Argentine parties. Some feel, for example, that there is a serious lack of representativeness in the party system as a whole; and that the Revolutionary Junta's dissolution of parties in 1966 was warranted. There are different shades of opinion in regard to just how representative Argentine parties really are. A former Argentine President feels that the political parties are representative to the extent that their leaders represent the interests and ideas of determinant social and economic groups. Then, there is the opinion of Peronist militants who maintain that it is the Justicialist Party that is an authentic representation of all strata of the Argentine citizenry.

There is a tendency in political science to associate the problem of representativeness with the electoral system of proportional representation. The author feels, however, that, like oil and water, the two will not mix, that the proportional system will inevitably lead to the atomization of parties and will decrease the chances for the formation of stable majorities. In opposition to the system of proportional representation adopted in 1963, strong support still exists for the defunct Saenz Peña Law (an attempt to develop a two-party system) on the premise that this arrangement would be more conducive to a really representative, homogeneous majority.

The over-all functional role of the party system in Argentina is another popular target for criticism. According to Castagno, Argentine parties do not perform effectively as agencies of political socialization (a process which involves the shaping of a citizen's attitudes toward the political system, whether the political system be totalitarian or democratic) because they regard their electoral function as more important than all else. For Castagno, it would seem more important for Argentine parties to function as a mechanism for the process of inculcating democratic values in the Argentine citizenry.[8] Bidart Campos makes the point that political parties in Argentina have not managed to articulate the diversity of heterogeneous interests, much less to stabilize them in any harmonious way.[9] Accordingly, political behavior on the part of the citizenry at the polls tends to be mechanical and meaningless. The pattern of voting behavior indicates that the citizen at the polls will vote for the party that represents the least of all evils, for the party that least displeases him, but paradoxically less frequently for the party with which he is fully satisfied.[10]

The apparent weakness of Argentine party structures lies in their inability to accommodate partisan aims to specific or general demands in the polity. In this view one may attribute the political influence of pressure groups to the inefficacy of political parties; the pressure groups are "pinch-hitting" for parties in Argentina, and in all likelihood will continue to do so until parties are able to aggregate the multifarious interests of the polity satisfactorily.[11]

The divisive nature of internal party politics is often singled out as a major factor contributing to party inefficiency. Political parties are frequently plagued with bitter power struggles which block their normal activity in the political system. Party leaders seem to agree that one of the major defects of party structures is the absence of an effective democratic internal mechanism capable of providing political orientation to citizen and party member alike. Participation of the citizenry in the internal life of the parties is for the most part scant and sporadic. This condition is partly due to the stipulation in the Law of Political Parties which restricts participation in the internal life of the party to affiliates (or registered members) only.[12] General disinterest coupled with the attitude that politics is a "dirty" process also tends to discourage active involvement within the parties on the part of the citizenry.

Dissatisfaction with the party system in Argentina is sometimes attributed to the fractionalized nature of party structures, which further inhibits their capacity to mobilize opinion and the electorate. As we have seen, the system comprises an impressive array of political parties and groups which have developed not so much because of a real necessity but more because of the process of atomization resulting from local struggles within the political community. These struggles cannot be divorced from the *caudillistic* syndrome which has prevailed in Argentina since independence.

CAUDILLISMO

The two political parties that divided the country in the nineteenth century were the *Unitarios* of Buenos Aires, revolutionary and progressive, emulating the French in general and especially Rousseau and Montesquieu; and on the other side the *Federales* represented by Córdoba, conservative and opposed to change, Spanish in education, religion, and literature.[13] These parties emerged from the ideas and struggles of their various *caudillos*.

Traditional *caudillismo* flourished in the days of José Artigas, Estanislao López, Francisco Ramírez, Juan Bautista Bustos, Felipe Varela, and Juan Facundo Quiroga.[14] Most of these *caudillos* were wealthy *estancieros* ("landowners") who depended on personalism, charisma, and at times the gauchos, to maintain their power. They were characterized by their ruthlessness at both the provincial and national levels to insure their political continuity.

The *caudillistic* pattern which developed is sometimes attributed to the feeling of social alienation experienced by the immigrants and early settlers. There was a great need on the part of these people for some central authority to regulate their political life and provide them with security. This situation ushered in the *patrón–péon* psychology where the strong held sway over the weak.

With the coming of industrialization in the early twentieth century, *caudillismo* served to provide a unifying symbolism for such political parties as the *Radicales,* as personified in the leadership of Irigoyen, and the *Peronistas* as represented by Juan Perón.

The numerous parties which have taken shape over the years have tended to shade off with a certain degree of overlapping into four broad ideological categories: conservatism, radicalism, socialism, and peronism.

CONSERVATISM

A group of conservative-oriented parties formed the *Federación Nacional de Partidos de Centro* (FNPC) that basically represents the landed elite and traditional oligarchic interests in Argentina.[15] The conservative doctrine supports the idea of progress, the moral principles of Christianity, individual awareness of social responsibilities, respect for the traditions and customs of the past, free enterprise and private intiative, democracy based on a representative formula, minority rights, federalism, and the viability of the national constitution.

RADICALISM

Generally, middle-class-oriented parties tended to rally 'round the flag of Argentine radicalism and its basic philosophy of political democracy.[16] The two foremost representatives of radicalism today are the *Unión Cívica Radical Intransigente* (UCRI) and the *Unión Cívica Radical del Pueblo* (UCRP). The attitudes of both parties toward the problems of development reflect a protectionist nationalism conditioned by the traditional struggles between the forces of the interior and the port.

An interesting offshoot of the Radical Intransigent party is the development-oriented *Movimiento de Integración y Desarrollo* (MID) founded by former President Frondizi in 1964. The MID, like the *Partido Demócrata Cristiano* and *Partido Demócrata Progresista,* proffers a pragmatic, integrationist view of politics; but, like other political groupings in Argentina, it is not free of factionalism within its ranks.[17]

SOCIALISM

The splintering process seems to have played the most havoc in the Socialist Party. It is safe to say that no Argentine party has suffered more schisms in its entire life span. Thus, whenever one mentions socialism in regard to Argentine parties it is necessary to specify whether the reference is, for example, to the *Partido Socialista Internacional* (the Argentine Communist Party)[18] the *Socialistas Independientes,* the *Socialistas Obreros,* the *Partido Socialista Argentino,* the *Partido Socialista Democrático,* or to others which have appeared in the politics of the country.[19]

Related to this split in the ranks of the Socialist Party is the problem which has perplexed other parties in the Argentine political spectrum as well, namely, that of adjusting party structures to the demands of modernization without prostituting party ideology.[20] No Argentine party has been able to sidestep this problem and, sadly, no workable solution is in sight.

PERONISM

The modernizing influence has also plagued peronism as divisively as it has other parties in the political picture. In the Argentina since the fall of Perón, it is no longer possible to describe the Peronist party as a rigid, doctrinal structure which does not tolerate *any* factionalism within its ranks.[21] Divisionist elements, however, do not seem to pose a serious threat to the unitary structure of the organization, which continues to be controlled from Madrid. The preponderant influence of Perón was clearly demonstrated in the Mendoza gubernatorial elections in 1966. Here, to the surprise of all, Perón engineered the victory of the "Peronist" candidate over the "Vandorist" representative.[22] This election also raised speculation regarding the ephemeral character of the Peronist split when the divided Peronist camp decided to forget differences and combine forces in order to defeat the opposition and further the Peronist cause.

Thus, the entire process of divisionism and political cleavage within the movement is suspect. Some consider the internal party struggle as a deliberate effort on the part of the Peronist Caesar in Madrid to divide in order to conquer. A more prevalent view is that the divisionist syndrome is real and a genuine reaction to the forces of modernization in Argentina. To meet the rugged demands of modernism, a significant sector of the Peronist elites feels that their process of leadership selection must be revamped to provide for the democratic selection of a capable cadre of leaders. These views of course make for conflict with the desiderata of Perón who is reluctant to impersonalize the system of leadership selection. Thus there are two contrasting views which would obviously make for dissidence. The author queried Peronist leaders as to whether or not Peronist doctrine has changed over the years. The general response reads something like this: Perón is their leader, that must be understood, but, the doctrine is not the same doctrine as in 1955; it is being modernized to cope with changing times. In the words of one of the labor leaders: *el Peronismo se está actualizando.* While they will readily admit that Perón is their boss, they are quick to point out that he is out of touch with the new *dirigentes* and as a result has committed many a blunder in dealing with them.

The wave of Peronist divisionism also suggests the interesting hypothesis that the Peronist movement is disintegrating. It is of course difficult to test this supposition empirically. Still, there are counter hypotheses which should be considered in evaluating the over-all prospects of survival of the movement. First, it cannot be overlooked that peronism embraces in its ideology a general commitment to modernization—a concept which represents the general aspirations of the Argentine masses, and which obviously cannot be obliterated by decree for it involves the entire idea of industrialization upon which the nation-building process rests. In order simply to destroy the movement, it would be necessary to destroy the concept of industrialization; this is not likely to occur. Second, *peronism* portrays an image of economic success and well-being for the nation which tends to integrate rather than disintegrate general support for its cause. Third, the Peronist movement is bolstered by the unifying charisma and leadership of Juan Perón himself who still commands the respect of the alienated masses seeking incorporation into the national community.

Furthermore, one cannot overlook the want-satisfying function the Peronist movement served in its heyday. Perón filled a certain basic economic need during the ten years of his rule, and the governments that came after him are somehow not considered in the eyes of the people to have measured up to his accomplishments. In Argentine circles (Peronist and non-Peronist) the point is often made that the Peronist movement is not disintegrating, notwithstanding the intramovement conflict among different leaders; that the Peronist movement continues to be vertically and efficiently organized, making the mandates of Perón the order of the day; and that Juan Perón is still the power figure in the movement.

In terms of what has been said, the disintegration hypothesis regarding the Peronist movement is tenuous. What must be kept in mind is that *peronismo* is able to reach the masses in spite of the structures. This simple statement indicates the present course of Peronist tactics. Perón for all intents and purposes is the *Caudillo Máximo*. The structures of the Peronist movement are used as channels for Perón's energy to be infused into the system. This at least represents the old traditional organization of the movement. From all indications the great power of Perón lies in his ability to veto decisions contrary to his liking as he did in the Mendoza case.

There is no doubt that an internal struggle is in process, but this is not to be viewed as a division within *peronismo*. What is going on could best be described perhaps as a clash between the old and the new, between tradition and modernity, between structure and superstructure.[23] In the current power structure some labor leaders appear to be pitted against the leadership of Perón. In the author's view, internal difficulties within the movement basically stem from general dissatisfaction among the *dirigentes* or "leaders" regarding their position in the leadership hierarchy of the movement. In this respect, the internal problems are considered ephemeral, inasmuch as they do not affect the masses upon which the entire movement is based.

It is felt that the masses remain indifferent to the power struggle within local leadership. In other words, leaders can come to blows in quarreling among themselves, but in reality it is the one leader (Perón) and the masses he controls that count. The masses still obey Perón, no matter if the *dirigentes* are fighting among themselves.[24] It can be theorized, then, that the disintegration of *peronismo* in Argentina remains to be realized. The continuing quarrels within the local leadership of the movement and the cropping up of dissident Peronists point to the presence of the disrupting force of modernization which has taken its toll in schisms in other parties and political groups as well. As regards *peronismo,* the problem is the same for Onganía as it was for Illia: *Peronismo* is a political reality; it cannot be swept under the rug or hidden in closets. In the interest of political stability, it must be integrated into Argentine political life.

POLITICAL INTEGRATION IN THE PARTY SYSTEM

It has been difficult for the political elites of various parties who spearhead the political development movement to introduce a working multiparty system in Argentina. Instead, the party system has been characterized by a blatant form of resistance to mobilization into broad fronts in support of the goals of nation-building. On the other hand, however, a certain degree of political integration in the party system was evidenced prior to the 1966 coup. The Argentine electorate formed around the Peronist vis-à-vis the anti-Peronist banners. This arrangement of major political fronts could be observed in several electoral contests. For example, in the elections of the province of San Juan in 1965, the *Unión Cívica Radical del Pueblo* (UCRP) joined forces with the *Unión Cívica Radical Bloquista* (UCRB) to form the anti-Peronist coalition which defeated the Peronist grouping by a substantial margin. Again, in the 1965 communal elections in Posadas, capital of the province of Misiones, the formation into major political fronts was observed when the anti-Peronist bloc formed by the UCRP and the *Frente Comunal* lost to the Peronists. The situation repeated itself in the 1965 municipal elections in the Province of Río Negro which saw the anti-Peronist bloc, mainly represented by the UCRP, win over the Peronist force. The 1966 provincial elections in Jujuy and Mendoza also indicated a casting of votes into the Peronist–anti-Peronist clusters. After the March 1965 congressional elections, the Peronists were just about evenly matched in the Chamber of Deputies against their principal anti-Peronist opposition, the UCRP.[25]

This phenomenon of major political front formations, sometimes pejoratively labeled *política de opción,* is regarded with optimism in certain Argentine circles. Some political elites will point out that there is no alternative to the two-party arrangement to insure a viable form of democratic politics in Argentina. Thus, mobilization of the electorate into two political fronts corresponding to the Peronist and non-Peronist elements is regarded as a promising step in the right direction. In an interview with an Argentine legislator, the interesting hypothesis was put to the author that, as Argentina slowly develops economically, a two-party or two-front arrangement will inevitably emerge in the political system. Rather than two tightly disciplined parties in opposition there would be two broad fronts of parties aligned because of economic necessity against each other, each espousing a different economic doctrine.

A less optimistic, but perhaps more realistic, thesis is that a two-party or two-front system in Argentina hardly warrants speculation. The prospects of developing a two-front arrangement would seem to diminish when one considers the high level of heterogeneity in opinions and beliefs among individuals comprising the body politic, not to mention the formidable problem of attempting to consolidate these diverse attitudes under one or two banners. It is known that Argentine individualism is a rugged individualism which will not conform to ideological alternatives. It is thus difficult to envisage in the political spectrum two political groups of parties sufficiently capable of integrating the divergent attitudes of the Argentine people. It would seem more likely that one will continue to find a proliferation of groups, and that these will continue to multiply rather than to jell into two streams of political opinion.

With the dissolution of political parties in Argentina it has been difficult to follow the pattern of party front formations in Argentine politics. There is a strong possibility that this phenomenon will continue to pervade the political process, simply because the conditions of political alienation still exist in the country. There is a certain psychology behind the formation of major party fronts which makes it thrive in an environment where fear, insecurity, and general political frustration are endemic in the political system.

This psychology of party front formation is usually relied upon by the dominant "minority" (be it *Radicalism* or *Peronism*) when it tends to put before the voter two alternatives according to which he must choose by reason either of fear or of preference. For example, it might be assumed that the Peronists in their politicization campaign will tell the voters that if they do not opt for their candidates at the polls they are in fact voting for that which represents rule by an oligarchy indifferent to the needs of the masses or the poor. The anti-Peronists, on the other hand, would try to persuade the voters not to vote for the Peronists unless they favored the return of a strong dictatorial government ruled by force.

It is hard to say whether or not these arguments satisfy the ideological or philosophical beliefs of the major part of the electorate. Still, a large number of parties, though diametrically opposed to the anti-Peronist segment, have been willing to sacrifice their political beliefs in order to side with the anti-Peronist party at the polls, thus allaying fears of the possibility of the return to the dictatorship that Perón personifies in their minds. This in capsule form is a manifestation of the psychology of major political fronts. When the Onganía government restores the electoral process to Argentina, it will be interesting to observe whether the Argentine people will then vote according to a criterion of fear rather than one of authentic preference.

THE THIRD NATIONAL FRONT

There are some sectors in the Argentine electorate which are reluctant to be boxed in by an either-or political alternative. The political dissatisfaction in this sector is gradually being channeled toward the consolidation of the *tercera fuerza nacional* or third national force, capable of absorbing that significant segment of the population which prefers to remain aloof from the Peronist–anti-Peronist dilemma. The followers of former president Frondizi have been the leading exponents of this popular-front idea, but to date the realization of their objectives is still a distant dream.[26] It should be pointed out that the *tercerista* or third-front idea has not been discounted and continues to be cultivated among the *acuerdistas* or alliance-oriented groups as a solid approach toward the normalization of Argentine politics.

INTRAPARTY RECRUITMENT

It is important to compare party structures in a political system in relation to the manner in which they carry out the political function of leadership selection. According to the sociologist José Luis de Imaz, no uniform criteria exist for the recruitment of leadership groups within the party structures in Argentina; there are as many criteria as there are parties and in the final analysis the different modes of selection are determined by the ideology of each party.[27] This heterogeneous pattern is explained by the lack of consensus which exists in the Argentine political system and is contrasted with the more stable systems, such as the United States, where political consensus permits similar techniques of selection to be employed regardless of party ideology.[28]

In the Argentine political system there are both latent and manifest styles attending the process of selection within the respective parties. The latent pattern is basically ascription-oriented, assigning high priority to personalistic rather than achievement criteria in the selection of party candidates for high office. On the other hand the manifest style is geared to the organic law of political parties which up until the Coup of 1966 provided the general format to be followed by all recognized political parties in their selection processes. Manifestly, all recognized parties were known to comply with the legal stipulation that "they will practice in their internal life the democratic system through periodic elections for the nomination of authorities and candidates, through the participation of affiliates in conformity with the prescriptions of their organic charters." [29] Thus, every political party has an organic charter tailored according to stipulations of the party statute for the purpose of selecting its candidates for public and party office. To protect their "legal personality," parties in their selection activity tend to stay within or remain as close as possible to the law. More interesting however, is the less manifest, latent pattern of recruitment about which little has been written mainly because of its *sub rosa* quality. What the author was able to ascertain in this regard derives mainly from interviews with knowledgeable persons both within and outside party circles.

In analyzing the latent aspect of recruitment, it must be assumed that a certain degree of manipulation of the members by different internal elements within the party is always present. As a result, the organic system of selection established in accordance with the Law of Political Parties is not necessarily foolproof; the organic charters of the different parties simply do not take into account (purposely or not) internal factors such as *caudillism,* personalism, kinship ties, and other similar variables which exercise an important role in the intraparty decision-making process. The problem of personalism, as in the formation of political groupings around a personality, is common to both large and small parties and tends to inhibit the operation of any kind of formalized recruitment system. In the provinces, there is the element of *bloquismo* or political bloc formations operating within the *caudillismo* framework which heavily influences the ultimate result of selection procedures notwithstanding the formality of the secret ballot and other institutional measures.

It is also important to note that only a very small portion of the citizenry enroll themselves in the Argentine political parties. According to the hypothesis of latent recruitment elaborated to the author during his stay in Argentina, the small minority which enrolls in the traditional parties does not do so spontaneously but is motivated by certain small leaders, commonly called in the political vernacular *los punteros,*[30] who because of some *compromiso,* or arrangement with a party boss, go about enrolling people in these parties. The point is that the people do not sign up because of personal belief in the parties; (in many instances their beliefs are contrary to those of the party in which they enroll) but are lured by promises and sometimes actual fulfillment of their immediate needs by the *puntero*.

On the theme of latent recruitment, it may be useful to divide the parties into three broad sectors: first, the old traditional parties, mainly those which preceded the Peronists and have continued to exist up to the present time; second, those pertaining to peronism which exhibit a special kind of recruitment process distinct from the traditional parties; and third, parties which adhere to an ideology and conform to this ideology in their activities.

Parties of the first type are commonly called democratic and have developed from a liberalist root. The Radical Party and the Conservative Party are the two main traditional parties which dominated the first part of the century until the appearance of *peronismo* in the aftermath of the Second World War. Those parties to which the traditional label can be applied do not support a strong ideology; their base is their liberalism, and they are essentially large electoral parties.

In the traditional party the most active person is not the average party member but the *puntero*. Party leaders of this class are presumably the first to cast their votes for or against the prospective candidate in the internal elections of the party. The function of the *puntero* is to mobilize and maintain, with his power of patronage, an electoral clientele. His influence is in direct proportion to his patronage potential. The *puntero* system is to be found at municipal, state, and national levels of the political system. Accordingly, each *puntero* has his *puntos,* as his followers are pejoratively labeled, whose responsibility is to participate at the discretion of the *puntero* in the elections which select party authorities and candidates for public office. It is assumed that the *punteros* have considerable bargaining power, in some respects even more than the *caudillo* within the party structure who must curry their favor to get his party list elected to office.

The electoral mechanism as it operates within the traditional party can be understood as a consequence of alliances (or *trenzas* as they are called) of *punteros* among themselves who together agree to support a *caudillo* and his slate of candidates. In turn, the *caudillos* of the parties may ally themselves to elect to particular posts such major leaders as are deemed suitable and mutually acceptable. This process, although generally associated with the traditional parties, is also to be found, perhaps under a different guise, in other parties. It is a mechanism which one can safely say is completing its cycle in Argentina and gradually disappearing with the influence of modernization in the political process.

Peronismo introduces the second category in the typology of latent recruitment styles. The appearance of *peronismo* is an expression of the modernization process in the Argentine society, the roots of which stem in turn from a process of industrialization. *Peronismo* is considered a new force which does not have any characteristics of the two major traditional parties. It is not run on the basis of the party machine, which in sum represents a *modus operandi* to promote the recruitment of vested candidates in intraparty or public elections; but is instead a multitudinal movement which has only one boss who sits by himself with pen and paper and designates candidates of his preference. There are no internal partisan elections nor any kind of formalized recruitment process—no party machine nor *caudillos*. The boss, Perón, simply appoints and afterwards goes about establishing certain formalities to comply with the minimal requirements of the law. Accordingly, candidates are signed up as representatives of the Peronist party, but, from all indications, the party functions merely as a pseudoparty with respect to the role and performance of other political parties in the system.

All Peronists are on Perón's side and the dealings of Perón with them are direct through modern mass communication media —prior to his exile through the use of radio and newspapers and personal appearance, and now by means of recorded messages, letters, and personal emissaries from Madrid. There is no doubt that the Peronist organization is of the mass type, where leaders are simply a formality. Perón hires and fires the "leaders" with a simple twist of the thumb because in reality there are no inter-mediate levels of organization. There are just Perón and the masses, and his style of recruitment, commonly called in Argentina *digitación*, or literally "appointment by the finger," is a purely personal one.

The third sector which has been distinguished from the other two generally corresponds to the group of ideological parties vis-à-vis those formally described as conservative and radical. These parties existed prior to the epoch of Perón and can be generally described as of the left wing. Taking into account that there have been several subdivisions, the ideological parties neverthe-less belong to two main groupings in Argentina: socialism and communism. In both parties the process of political recruitment is carried out on an ideological basis, and there are relatively no *caudillos*. A high level of militancy is exhibited in these parties and the membership is participant and indoctrinated. Leadership in the socialist ranks is exercised at different levels and tends to be intellectually rather than electorally oriented, as compared with the party machine of the *caudillos*. The socialist movement more or less revolves around the intellectual leadership of such notables as Alfredo Palacios (now deceased), Américo Ghioldi, and Alicia Moreau de Justo. The Communist party is organized along more or less the same lines but its overt participation in the political process is proscribed. Parties belonging to the ideo-logical sector do not accept the political recruitment system of the traditional electoral parties but function instead according to more programmatic and disciplined methods to select their membership and those who will possibly represent them in gov-ernment office.

REFLECTIONS ON RECRUITMENT MECHANISMS

There are several theories as to why the traditional mecha-nisms of recruitment, namely, the *puntero* and party machine system, have tended to deteriorate. It is argued that the process of modernization, which has given birth to an industrial pro-letariat with typical syndicalist leanings, is largely responsible.

The assumption here is that this new industrial sector of the citizenry, formerly protected by the *puntero* of the party, now seeks protection in the syndicalist structure. The syndicate with its tremendous political influence and patronage power is capable of assuming the role of the *caudillo* on a more extensive scale, thus liberating the citizen from the tutelage of the *caudillo*.

The rise in standard of living concurrent with the industrialization process in Argentina is often regarded as another important factor in the decline of the traditional mechanism of recruitment. As the economic condition of the downtrodden individual improves he is better able to resolve his own personal problems without the aid or protection of the *caudillo*. The citizen, in other words, increases his bargaining power with direct protection of the syndicate in which it behooves him to become an active participant. The situation is now one in which the *caudillo* finds himself without a clientele to maximize his aims in the recruitment process. This new dimension of autonomy and liberty to a certain extent enables the masses to break the umbilical cord from the *caudillos* of the old traditional party structures.

There has also been noted a modernization of attitudes among the leaders of other parties, who now seek a direct means of communication with the masses, thus breaking away from the old party machine tendencies. The foremost exponent of this new approach is Arturo Frondizi. It should be mentioned that Frondizi has not succeeded in freeing himself altogether from the party machine because political expediencies still demand that the party machine exist. This is especially the case in those areas, such as the backward provinces, where industrialization has not made inroads. Here the party apparatus functions in a traditional way. It is interesting to point out in this regard the apparent correlation between industrialization and the modernization of party structures in Argentina. In the zones where industrialization has developed—for example, in the provinces of Buenos Aires and the littoral—there are indications that the party machine is gradually deteriorating and is being replaced by the syndicates as an expression of political power. In contrast, in the provinces where little or no industry exists—Corrientes,

Catamarca, Entre Ríos, for example—the old party machine continues to be a viable force.

As mentioned earlier, the so-called traditional parties were also seeking ways, up until the Revolution of '66, to modernize their party structures. An interesting modernization scheme in Frondizi's party, the MID (*Movimiento de Integración y Desarrollo*), divided the Federal Capital, which comprises 20 *parroquias* or electoral districts, into 209 small circuits, each comprising a small number of citizens who are all well known to each other and not dependent upon a *caudillo*. The idea behind this arrangement was to encourage greater participation of the bases of the party through each of these circuits, and to avoid interference by the *caudillo* whose support-building potential was severely curtailed in small districts. The plan was never really put to the test, and it is doubtful whether it would have significantly obscured the presence of the traditional *caudillo*. Still, it can be viewed as an attempt to modify a recruitment practice that is now generally frowned upon in Argentina.

In the light of the disillusionment of political parties in 1966, it would seem that the fundamental problem confronting the Onganía regime would be how to create a democratic culture without political parties. The general speculation is that the dissolution of political parties will prove to have been but a steppingstone to the creation of new parties, perhaps oriented toward development as is the MID (*Movimiento de Integración y Desarrollo*).[31] What has been anticipated in other quarters is the emergence of a dominant post-Revolutionary party, somewhat along the lines of the *Partido Revolucionario Institucional* (PRI) in Mexico,[32] which will be able to provide cohesion to classes and sectors alike in order to further the goals of modernization in the country. For the present, neither of these aspirations has been fulfilled. On the contrary, the political parties remain disorganized, divided, and devoid of any constitutional public function.

NOTES

1. Bidart Campos, "Fuerzas Políticas en el Régimen Constitucional Argentino," p. 901.
2. César Enrique Romero, "Problemática del Partido Político," p. 74. (Author's translation.)
3. *Ibid.*
4. For some interesting studies of political parties in Argentina, see Campobassi *et al.*, *Los Partidos Políticos, Estructura y Vigencia en la Argentina.*
5. Romero, *op. cit.*, p. 75.
6. See Article 47 of the Constitution of the Province of Entre Ríos, Article 85 of the Constitution of the Province of Chaco, Articles 237 and 242 of the Constitution of the Province of Chubut, Article 28 of the Constitution of the Province of Neuquén, Article 14 of the Constitution of the Province of Río Negro.
7. Antonio Castagno, *Los Partidos Políticos Argentinos,* pp. 8, 117.
8. *Ibid.,* pp. 130–131.
9. Bidart Campos, *Grupos de Presión y Factores de Poder,* p. 110.
10. *Ibid.,* pp. 110–111.
11. Alfredo Galletti, *La Realidad Argentina en el Siglo XX,* Tomo I, *La Política y Los Partidos,* p. 246.
12. *Ley de Los Partidos Políticos, No. 16.652,* Article 35.
13. See Sarmiento, "Life in the Argentine Republic: Civilization or Barbarism," tr. Mrs. Horace Mann, in *Why Perón Came to Power,* p. 50.
14. For an excellent discussion on some of the more prominent *caudillos* in Argentina, see Luna, *Los Caudillos.*
15. For the political doctrine and beliefs of this coalition, see *Soluciones Conservadoras 1962, passim.*
16. Some highlights of Argentine radicalism are elaborated in del Mazo, *El Radicalismo: Notas Sobre su Historia y Doctrina, 1922–1952,* and *El Radicalismo: El Movimiento de Intransigencia y Renovación, 1945–1957;* see also Snow, *Argentine Radicalism: The History and Doctrine of the Radical Civic Union, passim.*
17. See Cortés Conde, "Partidos Políticos," in *Argentina 1930–1960;* Carlos S. Fayt, "La Organización Interna de los Partidos y los

Métodos Políticos en la Argentina," in Campobassi *et al., Los Partidos Políticos.*

18. The name "Argentine Communist Party" was adopted in 1920; see Alexander, *Communism in Latin America,* Chapter IX.

19. See Marianetti, *Argentina, Realidad y Perspectivas,* pp. 374–386.

20. For notes on the doctrinal base of the party, see Ghioldi, *Juan B. Justo, passim;* Luis Pan, *Justo y Marx, passim.*

21. According to the Peronist Manual, factionalism within the party is clearly not permitted. See *Manual del Peronista,* p. 129.

22. The "Peronist" party bloc corresponded to the so-called orthodox line represented by Perón's third wife, María Estela Martínez de Perón. The "Justicialist" bloc, on the other hand, represented the "Vandorist" position of Augusto Vandor who was assassinated in 1969. In the Mendoza elections in 1966, Perón successfully ran a "black horse" against the popular Vandorist candidate allegedly to show the dissident Peronist leaders who was boss. See *La Nación,* April 19, 1966.

23. See Grondona, "Después de Mendoza," p. 7.

24. Peronists in general manifest blind obedience to the "conductor," Juan Perón. This obedience was especially put to the test in the early part of 1966 when the political activity of Isabelita (Perón's third wife) began to have repercussions within the movement. Interviews with several party militants around that time revealed their unflinching faith in Isabelita, notwithstanding their interpretation of her abrupt measures in regard to the hiring and firing of some of their number as deliberate moves to disintegrate the cohesive stand of the party organization. Some Peronists admitted they were in the dark regarding the true purpose of her visit but at the same time believed that as Perón's emissary she was undoubtedly "fulfilling a mission." In the words of one Peronist, "The General does not always show his hand but he has his reasons."

25. The Peronists had a total of 51 seats against 74 for the UCRP.

26. The willingness of diverse political groups to give this "third front" idea a chance was manifested in the signing of the *acuerdo de Posadas,* which was in essence an agreement among different political parties to pool their votes to offset the polarization phenomenon in a municipal election.

27. de Imaz, *Los Que Mandan,* p. 196.

28. *Ibid.,* pp. 196–197; in the Argentine process, Imaz observes the presence of both formal and informal styles of selection and singles out the latter as the most interesting for study.

29. See *Ley de los Partidos Políticos,* No. 16.652, p. 8.

30. For a polemic discussion of this operation, see Bianchin, *Qué Hacer Con los Partidos Políticos?* Chapter IX.

31. "Sin Partidos Hacia Nuevos Partidos," p. 1710.

32. For some scholarly appraisals of Mexico's one-party system, see Padgett, *The Mexican Political System;* Scott, *Mexican Government in Transition,* Chapters 5 and 6; Cline, *Mexico: Revolution to Evolution 1940–1960; Fernández, Political Administration in Mexico.*

CHAPTER 5

TENTATIVE PATTERNS
OF POLITICAL
ELITE RECRUITMENT

In order to examine patterns of recruitment in Argentina, we shall assume the country to have reached a sufficient degree of differentiation to permit study of the political elite. This elite should be distinguished from other elites in the power structure such as business leaders or landed aristocrats. Furthermore, it is important to bear in mind that elites do not spontaneously appear in the political universe but are produced by the existing political socialization processes within the system. These political socialization efforts are largely characterized by the growth of manifest, specialized institutions performing political orientation functions likely to affect the environment and attitudes of the political elite.

Although there is some variation from country to country, one able observer posits the following profile as most character-istic of political elite recruitment for the Latin American con-text: In both government and party posts the creole or "white"

group tends to predominate; the forces of economic modernization facilitate political mobility for new or disenfranchised sectors of the citizenry; formal education often becomes a defini-
tional characteristic of the elite; the achievement of commissioned
status in the military ranks as well as strong religious ties with
the Catholic Church may be central considerations for recruitment to government positions. In a number of Latin American
countries, political groups organized along the lines familiar to
western Europe and the United States, recruit personnel.[1] This
is the case specifically in Argentina where the party system has
been found to be the principal agent in the political selection
process. The variables enumerated above point up some of the
avenues the researcher may pursue in his analysis of the recruitment problem.[2]

THE CLASSIFICATORY SCHEME

In this book I will categorize the political elite in Argentina
in terms of three sectors—National Executive, Gubernatorial,
and Legislative. The National Executive Sector (NES) is operationally defined to include the President and Vice-President of
the Republic and Ministers and Secretaries of State; the Gubernatorial Sector includes the governors of the 22 states and the
territory of Tierra del Fuego; and the Legislative Sector comprises national Senators and Deputies. This categorization according to types and levels of office provides for intersectoral
comparisons.

By sector, the offices with which this study is chiefly concerned are the following: In the NES: President and Vice-President of the Republic, and the following Ministers: Labor and
Social Security, Foreign Relations and Worship, Economy, Works
and Public Services, National Defense, Interior, Agriculture, Education and Justice, Social Welfare and Public Health, Industry;
and Secretaries of State of Public Works, Finance, Commerce,
Treasury, Communications, Transportation, Navy, Air Force,
War, Energy and Combustibles. In 1958, this sector had a total

population of 27; five office holders resigned their posts and were replaced by five new office holders. In 1963, this sector had a population of 22.

The Gubernatorial Sector, as stated earlier, includes the governors of the 22 provinces and one territory. The total population for this sector in 1958 was 26; the provinces of Neuquén, Santa Cruz, and Formosa had two governors each during this period. The total population for 1963 was 24 with the province of Chubut having two governors.

In the Legislative Sector, comprising the offices of Senator and Deputy in the Argentine National Congress, there were 185 deputies and three vacant seats with the opening of Congress in 1958. One hundred new deputies were added to the Congress during the 1958 administration, making a total of 285 deputies. There were 42 senators and four vacant seats at the beginning of the 1958 administration; 18 senators were added to the Senate making a total of 60 senators. The total population for this sector in the 1958 administration was 345. The 1963 administration had 46 senators with one replacement. The National Congress opened in 1963 with a total of 192 deputies. Ninety-nine deputies were added to the Congress during the 1963 administration, making a total of 291.[3] The total population for this sector was 338.

FACTORS FOR ANALYSIS

Quantified biographical data on 782 members of the Argentine political elite for the period of study (398 for the 1958 administration and 384 for the 1963 administration) reveal certain variables in the recruitment process. These factors will be examined in terms of tendencies drawn from specific questions relevant to the recruitment function. The following questions were selected for examination with regard to the National Executive Sector: (1) Do members of the NES seem to be appointed on the basis of their professional "know-how"? (2) Is there a high turnover in one or more specific offices in the NES? And with regard to the Gubernatorial and Legislative Sectors: (3) Does the majority of the political elite come from the Central-Eastern region which includes the Port of Buenos Aires or from other regions of the country?

The following questions were asked in relation to all three sectors. (1) Is there a tendency for the political elite to begin on the national level and thus by-pass local and state offices? (2) Do the political elite return from the national level to state and local offices, or do they return to political inactivity? (3) Do the political elite tend to rise more through appointive than elective office? (4) Do the political elite tend to hold appointive rather than elective offices after occupying a NES or gubernatorial post? (5) Do the political elite serve in the Legislative Sector either before or after occupying a NES or gubernatorial post? (6) Is there a tendency for the political elite to "repeat" in a high office in one of the sectors? (7) How does "tenure of office" relate to age? (8) How do professional groupings figure in the recruitment process? For example, is there a predominance of lawyers and doctors in any one sector?

These questions will be discussed in terms of observable tendencies relating to relevant experience in office, regional representation, the level of education, the factor of age, occupational grouping, and the political activity index of the political elite.

TENTATIVE FINDINGS

Relevant Experience for Office

This variable relates to the appointment of members of the National Executive Sector on the basis of their professional "know-how." For operational purposes, qualifications were arbitrarily determined as follows:

Ministers
    of Social Welfare and Public   Doctor of Medicine
       Health
    of Education and Justice   Professor or Lawyer

of Industry	Economist or Industrialist
of Agriculture	Agricultural Engineer or Lawyer specializing in agrarian legislation
of Economy	Economist or Industrialist
of Foreign Relations and Worship	Diplomat or Ambassador
of the Interior	Lawyer
of National Defense	Military personnel
of Works and Public Services	Engineer
of Labor and Social Security	Lawyer or Economist

Secretaries

of Finance	Accountant or Economist
of Treasury	Accountant or Economist
of Communications	Engineer
of Transportation	Professor or Engineer
of Energy and Combustibles	Engineer
of War	Military personnel
of Navy	Naval personnel
of Air Force	Air Force personnel
of Commerce	Economist

As indicated in Table I, relevance of experience for office was regarded as an important criterion by both administrations in selecting the members who would occupy executive posts.

Regional Representation

Regional representativeness of the political elite is considered one of the more important desiderata in Argentina. Under this heading are included all the arguments regarding the interior versus the port and "who gets the most of what there is to get." As noted in Chapter 2 the antagonism between the *porteños* and the *provincianos* was evident even prior to Argentina's independence. As will be shown in the following tables, the interior

TABLE I
RELEVANCE OF EXPERIENCE FOR OFFICE IN THE
NATIONAL EXECUTIVE SECTOR

	1958		1963	
Experience	No.	Per cent	No.	Per cent
Relevant for NES office held	17	70.8	11	55.0
Not relevant for NES office held	7	29.2	9	45.0
Total	24	100.0	20	100.0

is as well represented, proportionately, by people from its own area as is the port.

Argentina's four major regions and the provinces which they comprise are as follows:

Region	Provinces	Approximate Population	Per cent of National Population
Central-Eastern	Buenos Aires Santa Fe Córdoba Entre Ríos San Luis La Pampa Federal Capital	14,500,000	73.0
Andean	Mendoza Tucumán Salta San Juan Jujuy Catamarca La Rioja Neuquén	3,000,000	14.0

	Corrientes Chaco		
Northern	Santiago del Estero	2,100,000	11.0
	Misiones		
	Formosa		
	Río Negro		
Southern	Chubut	400,000	< 2.5
	Santa Cruz		

The data show that the political elite in the National Executive Sector during the 1958 and 1963 administrations were recruited more from the Central-Eastern region than from other regions in the country. The over-all picture, however, shows the interior regions (Northern, Southern, and Andean) to be represented in decision-making posts in proportion to their approximate population. Politically, this points up a certain balance at the policy-making level and at the same time the broad geographic base from which those who govern tend to be selected.

Level of Education

A glance at Table III will clearly show that the Argentine political elite are highly educated—almost 50 per cent having at least some university education. As shown by the totals in the last column, the level of education of the elite from the two administrations compares quite favorably, with a maximum of 4 per cent difference between them. In connection with the recruitment process, education would seem to play an important part in all three sectors. Nearly all of the population included in this study displayed substantial educational background; that is, beyond the secondary level. This is not unusual, however, in a country such as Argentina where education is held at a high premium and is increasingly being regarded as one of the surest avenues to political success and mobility.

The Age Factor

Age is important in describing the political elite as it gives a general idea of the era to which they belong. It also provides

TABLE II
REGIONAL REPRESENTATION (BY BIRTH OF OFFICE HOLDERS)

	Central-Eastern Region		Northern Region		Southern Region		Andean Region		Unknown	
	No.	Per cent	No.	Per cent	No.	Per cent	No.	Per cent	No.	Per cent
(A) IN THE 1958 ADMINISTRATION										
National Executive (n = 27)	20	74.1	4	14.8	—	—	2	7.4	1	3.7
Gubernatorial (n = 26)	12	46.1	3	11.5	1	3.9	8	30.8	2	7.7
Legislative (n = 345)	157	45.5	28	8.1	5	1.5	29	8.4	126	36.5
Total (n = 398)	189	47.5	35	8.8	6	1.5	39	9.8	129	32.4

(B) IN THE 1963 ADMINISTRATION

National Executive (n = 22)	17	77.3	—	—	—	—	3	13.6	2	9.1
Gubernatorial (n = 24)	9	37.5	5	20.8	3	12.5	5	20.8	2	8.4
Legislative (n = 338)	153	45.3	19	5.6	6	1.8	27	8.0	133	39.3
Total (n = 384)	179	46.6	24	6.3	9	2.3	35	9.1	137	35.7

(C) PERCENTAGE OF OFFICE HOLDERS BORN IN EACH REGION WHO WERE ELECTED TO OFFICE FROM REGION OF BIRTH *

1958 Administration	87.7	71.0	100.0	94.6	—
1963 Administration	97.8	100.0	100.0	85.7	—

* The National Executive Sector is not included since its officials are appointed by the President to posts formally representing the interests of the entire country.

TABLE III
EDUCATIONAL BACKGROUNDS

Level of Education	National Executive Sector		Gubernatorial Sector		Legislative Sector		Total	
	No.	Per cent	No.	Per cent	No.	Per cent	No.	Per cent
(A) IN THE 1958 ADMINISTRATION								
Grade school	—	—	—	—	15	4.3	15	3.7
Attended secondary	—	—	—	—	3	.9	3	.8
Secondary school graduate	2	7.4	1	3.8	22	6.4	25	6.3
Attended university	3	11.1	1	3.8	27	7.8	31	7.8
University graduate	18	66.7	15	57.7	128	37.1	161	40.5
Graduate work	2	7.4	3	11.6	73	21.2	78	19.6
Unknown	2	7.4	6	23.1	77	22.3	85	21.3
Total	27	100.0	26	100.0	345	100.0	398	100.0

(B) IN THE 1963 ADMINISTRATION

Grade school	—	—	—	—	10	3.0	10	2.7
Attended secondary	—	—	3	12.5	1	.3	4	1.1
Secondary school graduate	—	—	2	8.3	30	8.9	32	8.4
Attended university	—	—	1	4.2	25	7.4	26	6.9
University graduate	17	77.3	13	54.1	140	41.4	170	45.2
Graduate work	4	18.2	1	4.2	55	16.3	60	16.0
Unknown	1	4.5	4	16.7	77	11.7	82	19.7
Total	22	100.0	24	100.0	338	100.0	384	100.0

a basis from which to formulate questions regarding (a) the adaptive behavior of the political elite toward issues of modernization, and (b) the extent to which political attitudes correlate with the youth or age of the members of governing bodies. In both administrations the majority of the political elite were under fifty as shown in Table IV.

Age appears to be an influencing factor affecting entrance into the political elite but, like education, tends to vary from sector to sector. The general tendency, however, seems to favor recruitment of younger men in all three sectors.

TABLE IV
REPRESENTATION BY AGE GROUP
IN THE 1958 AND 1963 ADMINISTRATIONS

Sector	1958		1963	
	No.	Per cent	No.	Per cent
National Executive				
(n = 27 in '58; 22 in '63)				
Under 50	13	48.2	9	40.9
Over 50	11	40.7	11	50.0
Unknown	3	11.1	2	9.1
Gubernatorial				
(n = 26 in '58; 24 in '63)				
Under 50	14	53.8	11	45.8
Over 50	10	38.5	11	45.8
Unknown	2	7.7	2	8.4
Legislative				
(n = 345 in '58; 338 in '63)				
Under 50	196	56.8	184	45.4
Over 50	131	38.0	130	38.5
Unknown	18	5.2	24	7.1
Total				
(n = 398 in '58; 384 in '63)				
Under 50	223	56.0	204	54.3
Over 50	152	38.2	152	40.4
Unknown	23	5.8	28	5.3

Occupational Grouping

The occupations of the political elite are arbitrarily broken down into the following classifications: Professional, Labor, Educational, Business, Dual,[4] and other. Tables V (A) and (B) indicate that in both administrations the majority of the political elite were professionals, with businessmen the second largest group. Those having held "dual" occupations are next on the scale. The majority of the elite who fall in this category are university professors who also practice law and doctors of jurisprudence who are university professors. Other "dual" occupations included journalists who were notaries public, lawyer-ranchers, and accountant-university professors. Table V(C) compares the total administrations by occupation.

A background in one of the professional occupations does not

TABLE V-A
OCCUPATIONAL REPRESENTATION
IN THE 1958 ADMINISTRATION

Occupations	National Executive Sector		Gubernatorial Sector		Legislative Sector	
	No.	Per cent	No.	Per cent	No.	Per cent
Professional						
Lawyer	6	22.2	11	42.4	83	24.1
Physician	1	3.7	4	15.4	54	15.7
Doctor of						
Jurisprudence	2	7.4	—	—	12	3.5
Engineer	—	—	—	—	4	1.2
Pharmacist	—	—	1	3.8	4	1.2
Biochemist	—	—	—	—	5	1.4
Dentist	—	—	—	—	2	.6
Economist	—	—	—	—	1	.3
Attorney General	—	—	—	—	1	.3
Publisher	—	—	—	—	1	.3

Labor						
Employee	—	—	—	—	11	3.2
Mechanic	—	—	—	—	1	.3
Educational						
Secondary teacher	—	—	—	—	15	4.3
University professor	—	—	—	—	3	.9
Business						
Public accountant	2	7.4	—	—	5	1.4
Realtor	—	—	—	—	6	1.7
Notary public	—	—	—	—	15	4.3
Merchant	—	—	3	11.6	36	10.4
Industrialist	—	—	—	—	9	2.6
Stockbroker	—	—	—	—	3	.9
Dual	10	37.1	1	3.8	27	7.8
Other						
Military	4	14.8	—	—	1	.3
Rancher	—	—	2	7.7	15	4.3
Journalist	—	—	2	7.7	7	2.0
Surveyor	—	—	—	—	1	.3
Photographer	—	—	—	—	1	.3
Law student	—	—	—	—	1	.3
Operations specialist	—	—	—	—	2	.6
Auctioneer	—	—	—	—	1	.3
Pharmaceutical salesman	—	—	—	—	1	.3
Petroleum technician	—	—	1	3.8	—	—
Unknown:	2	7.4	1	3.8	17	4.9
Total	27	100.0	26	100.0	345	100.0

appear to be the sole basis for recruitment to the political arena in Argentina; other criteria which the data do not reveal may include personal contacts, the "old school tie," or even perhaps "character," "integrity" or elusive "charisma," or other variables not necessarily oriented toward the achievement or performance criteria of the individual. Not to be discounted is the general tendency to show deference to professional training in the legal field. It is known that a government's possession of expertise contributes to effective policy-making; still, it is difficult to say what kind of expertise is best where policy is made and executed.

TABLE V-B
OCCUPATIONAL REPRESENTATION
IN THE ILLIA ADMINISTRATION

Occupations	National Executive Sector		Gubernatorial Sector		Legislative Sector	
	No.	Per cent	No.	Per cent	No.	Per cent
Professional						
Lawyer	7	31.9	8	33.3	99	29.2
Physician	2	9.1	2	8.3	38	11.1
Doctor of						
Jurisprudence	1	4.5	—	—	12	3.5
Engineer	1	4.5	1	4.2	6	1.7
Pharmacist	—	—	—	—	2	.6
Attorney General	—	—	—	—	2	.6
Dentist	—	—	—	—	6	1.7
Biochemist	—	—	—	—	4	1.2
Veterinarian	—	—	—	—	1	.3
Geologist	—	—	1	4.2	—	—
Labor						
Employee	—	—	—	—	33	9.8
Educational						
Secondary teacher	1	4.5	1	4.2	8	2.4
University professor	—	—	1	4.2	2	.6
Business						
Public accountant	—	—	—	—	5	1.5

Realtor	—	—	—	—	8	2.4
Notary public	—	—	—	—	11	3.3
Merchant	—	—	3	12.4	19	5.6
Industrialist	—	—	—	—	3	.9
Banker	—	—	1	4.2	1	.3
Sales manager	—	—	—	—	1	.3
Merchandiser	—	—	1	4.2	—	—
Dual	6	27.3	2	8.3	19	5.6
Other						
Military	2	9.1	—	—	18	5.4
Rancher	—	—	1	4.2	1	.3
Chemical technician	—	—	—	—	7	2.0
Journalist	—	—	—	—	1	.3
Sculptor	—	—	—	—	1	.3
Metallurgist	—	—	—	—	1	.3
Librarian	—	—	—	—	2	.6
Unknown	2	9.1	2	8.3	28	8.2
Total	22	100.0	24	100.0	338	100.0

Political Activity

The term "political activity" connotes circulation, whether by appointment or election, from one political office to another and thus the acquisition of political experience. This characteristic of the political elite is considered first in terms of those who entered the political office under study with or without prior political experience, as shown by comparison of the 1958 and 1963 administrations in Table VI(A). ("Political experience" is defined for purposes of this study to mean holding office in one or more of the capacities listed in the accompanying note.[5])

It is interesting to note that among the 14 in the NES of 1958 who had not held a political office before, two were re-

TABLE V-C
OCCUPATIONAL REPRESENTATION IN PER CENT
SUMMARIZED FOR THE 1958 AND 1963 ADMINISTRATIONS

Main Occupational Categories	1958	1963
Professional	48.2	50.0
Labor	3.0	8.5
Educational	4.5	3.6
Business	19.9	13.8
Other	9.8	8.8
Dual	9.6	7.0
Unknown	5.0	8.3
Total	100.0	100.0

TABLE VI-A
PRIOR POLITICAL EXPERIENCE
IN THE 1958 AND 1963 ADMINISTRATIONS

Sector	1958		1963	
	No.	Per cent	No.	Per cent
National Executive (n = 27 in 1958; 22 in 1963)				
Yes	13	48.2	14	63.7
No	14	51.8	7	31.8
Unknown	—	—	1	4.5
Gubernatorial (n = 26 in 1958; 24 in 1963)				
Yes	18	69.2	18	75.0
No	6	23.1	5	20.8
Unknown	2	7.7	1	4.2
Legislative (n = 345 in 1958; 338 in 1963)				
Yes	155	44.9	157	46.5
No	117	33.9	86	25.4
Unknown	73	21.2	95	28.1

cruited from business, three from the professional group, three were military men, and four had dual professions of lawyer-educator; the occupations of two of the 14 individuals were unknown. Among the seven without political experience in the 1963 National Executive Sector, one was an engineer, four were educators, and two were military men.

Of the six 1958 governors without prior political experience as defined here, two were from the professions, one was a merchant, one a journalist, one a petroleum technician, and one occupation was unknown. Of the five governors in the 1963 administration with no prior political experience, one was a lawyer, one a physician, one a professor, and two were businessmen.

The second index of political activity in the governing group is the by-passing by the political elite of state and local office on the way to their current posts, as presented in Table VI(B).

TABLE VI-B
BY-PASSING OF STATE AND LOCAL OFFICES
BY MEMBERS OF THE 1958 AND 1963 ADMINISTRATIONS

Sector	1958		1963	
	No.	Per cent	No.	Per cent
National Executive				
(n = 27 in 1958; 22 in 1963)				
Yes	19	70.4	15	68.2
No	8	29.6	6	27.3
Unknown	—	—	1	4.5
Gubernatorial				
(n = 26 in 1958; 24 in 1963)				
Yes	12	46.2	12	50.0
No	12	46.2	11	45.8
Unknown	2	7.7	1	4.2
Legislative				
(n = 345 in 1958; 338 in 1963)				
Yes	154	44.6	125	37.0
No	119	34.5	118	34.9
Unknown	72	20.9	95	28.1

In describing the political activity of the political elite, it is necessary to differentiate between appointive and elective offices in order to obtain a more comprehensive view of recruitment patterns in the political parties. Tables VI(C) and (D) indicate these distinctions at national and state levels for the two administrations; data for the local level are also shown although these cannot be differentiated quite so precisely.[6]

It is noteworthy that of the 27 members of the National Executive Sector for 1958 five held a national appointive office *in the subsequent administration.* Six legislators from the 1958 administration were appointed to national offices and two legislators occupied state appointive offices in the subsequent administration. One governor held a national elective office and two governors held a state elective office, forty-four legislators returned to hold a national elective office and six held state elective offices.

Table VI(E) shows a comparison of the types of office previously held by the total membership of the two administrations.

AN OVERVIEW OF RECRUITMENT PATTERNS

In terms of the political activity of those who attain high places in government, the pattern in all three sectors tends toward variety among individuals. The data show that political experience, as equated with some participation in political office either at the national, state, or local level, was not regarded as indispensable for successful political candidacy in any of the three sectors examined. Further, there is a tendency for prior political experience to have been more often in elective than appointive office in all three sectors. The so-called *hombre de relieve,* or "man of important standing," was often a top-draft choice for the decision-making agency of government, but many were also recruited from the ranks of those who had political experience. Neither was any one specific occupational or professional background a marked prerequisite for qualification to high office. Labor, education, and business occupations, to mention a few, were all part and parcel of the heterogeneous pool

TABLE VI-C
KINDS OF PRIOR POLITICAL EXPERIENCE
(BY LEVEL AND TYPE OF OFFICE HELD)
IN THE 1958 ADMINISTRATION

Sector	National Level		State Level		Local Level *	
	No.	Per cent	No.	Per cent	No.	Per cent
(1) APPOINTIVE OFFICE						
National Executive (*n* = 27)						
Yes	4	14.8	2	7.4		
No	23	85.2	25	92.6		
Gubernatorial (*n* = 26)						
Yes	1	3.8	—	—		
No	23	88.5	24	92.3		
Unknown	2	7.7	2	7.7		
Legislative (*n* = 345)						
Yes	5	1.4	16	4.6		
No	267	77.4	256	74.2		
Unknown	73	21.2	73	21.2		
(2) ELECTIVE OFFICE						
National Executive (*n* = 27)						
Yes	7	25.9	4	14.8	3	11.1
No	20	74.1	23	85.2	24	88.9
Gubernatorial (*n* = 26)						
Yes	5	19.2	9	34.6	4	15.4
No	19	73.1	15	57.7	20	76.9
Unknown	2	7.7	2	7.7	2	7.7
Legislative (*n* = 345)						
Yes	65	18.8	76	22.0	64	8.5
No	207	60.0	196	56.8	208	60.3
Unknown	73	21.2	73	21.2	73	21.2

* Offices included are Mayor and Councilman. The Mayor is ordinarily elected, but Councilmen may be either elected or appointed according to various local laws.

TABLE VI-D
KINDS OF PRIOR POLITICAL EXPERIENCE
(BY LEVEL AND TYPE OF OFFICE HELD)
IN THE 1963 ADMINISTRATION

Sector	National Level		State Level		Local Level *	
	No.	Per cent	No.	Per cent	No.	Per cent
(1) APPOINTIVE OFFICE						
National Executive (n = 22)						
Yes	3	13.7	2	9.1		
No	18	81.8	19	86.4		
Unknown	1	4.5	1	4.5		
Gubernatorial (n = 24)						
Yes	1	4.2	2	8.3		
No	22	91.8	21	87.5		
Unknown	1	4.2	1	4.2		
Legislative (n = 338)						
Yes	1	.3	24	7.1		
No	242	71.6	219	64.8		
Unknown	95	28.1	95	28.1		
(2) ELECTIVE OFFICE						
National Executive (n = 22)						
Yes	10	45.5	4	18.2	—	—
No	11	50.0	17	77.3	21	95.5
Unknown	1	4.5	1	4.5	1	4.5
Gubernatorial (n = 24)						
Yes	8	33.3	10	42.6	3	12.5
No	15	62.5	13	54.2	20	83.3
Unknown	1	4.2	1	4.2	1	4.2
Legislative (n = 338)						
Yes	73	21.6	83	24.6	50	14.8
No	170	50.3	160	47.3	193	57.1
Unknown	95	28.1	95	28.1	95	28.1

* Offices included are Mayor and Councilman. The Mayor is ordinarily elected, but Councilmen may be either elected or appointed according to various local laws.

TABLE VI-E
SUMMARY IN PER CENT OF PRIOR POLITICAL ACTIVITY
(BY LEVEL AND TYPE OF OFFICE HELD)
FOR THE 1958 AND 1963 ADMINISTRATIONS

	1958	1963
National appointive office	2.5	1.3
National elective office	19.3	23.7
State appointive office	4.5	7.3
State elective office	22.4	25.6
Local office	17.8	11.2
Any public office	46.7	49.2

from which political leaders were drawn. One may assume recruitment did not take place from any one privileged social stratum as is the case in certain countries in Europe.

In terms of what the data have revealed regarding the political elite for the period studied, the composite picture of the leadership structure in Argentina is encouraging. In this complex multiparty arrangement, recruitment takes place on a broad enough basis to seem to permit without undue regulation a successful operation of some form of democracy in the country. The leadership selected is a relatively young and highly educated group emerging indeed from a heterogeneous class but not devoid of the ability and expertise required in the critical role they must play in the decision-making process.

NOTES

1. Possible recruitment patterns for the entire Latin American context were formulated on the basis of Professor George I. Blanksten's criteria for the selection of new participants in Latin American politics. See "The Politics of Latin America," in Almond and Coleman, eds., *The Politics of the Developing Areas,* pp. 513–515.

2. For the Argentine case, the author draws on some of the propo-

sitions developed by C. Wright Mills in his attempt to identify the power elite on a national scale in the United States. The writer's investigation is more modest than that of Mills in its scope, and focuses on only a portion of the power elite: the political elite. See *The Power Elite*, p. 231.

3. The 99 deputies include three national deputies who assumed office in 1963 to fill vacancies left by the death of three deputies.

4. Dual occupations in the Argentine system are quite common, especially in the lawyer-professor ranks. This is due, in part, to the low salaries given to teachers and professors.

5. For operational purposes the offices listed below constitute political experience: At the national level—President, Vice-President, Cabinet Minister, Secretary of State, Ambassador, Federal Judge, National Deputy, National Senator. At the state level—Governor, Vice-Governor, State Minister, Chief of Police, State Deputy, State Senator. At the local level—Councilman and Mayor.

6. Appointive offices at the national level include Cabinet Ministers, Secretaries of State, Ambassadors, and Federal Judges; at the state level, State Ministers. Elective offices at the national level are President, Vice-President, National Deputy, and Senator; at the state level, Governor, Vice-Governor, Chief of Police, State Deputy, and Senator. The local offices used for this study are those of Mayor and Councilman. Since municipalities have no uniform electoral laws governing whether the post of Councilman is an elected or appointed office, these positions were used only to determine those of the political elite who had held a local office before entering one of the three sectors under investigation.

CHAPTER 6

POLITICAL ATTITUDES

For political development to be successful, the presence of a comparatively young, experienced, and enthusiastic elite capable of influencing the grounds on which decisions are made is simply not enough. In addition, the mobilization is required of human and economic resources necessary for the profitable implementation of national and international goals.

Although the dynamics of changing political systems can be studied in terms of the incidence of traditional norms, it is more important to observe the actual process of transition to modernity, particularly as reflected in attitudes regarding the change process [1] which are adopted by the political elites. A brief content analysis of discussions on the *recinto,* or "floor," of the Argentine National Congress, and declarations in meetings of the Alliance for Progress, Organization of American States, Latin American Free Trade Association, or the United Nations would clearly point up the ebullient nationalism which characterizes the Argentine style of politics.

One might define nationalism in the Argentine case as a political ideology which focuses on the preservation or maintenance of the nation-state. This definition has various ramifications

85

which points up one of the major problems which confronts the individual who ventures to apply the concept of nationalism to the study of political behavior in a particular country. In studying the politics of Argentina, the presence of nationalism cannot be avoided. The character which Argentine nationalism has assumed may perhaps be operationally explained as a type of "reactive nationalism," reacting positively toward all policies formulated to enhance national status, and reacting negatively toward forces which jeopardize the nation's autonomy, legitimacy, political organization, cohesiveness, and other related factors of national importance.[2]

METHOD OF ANALYSIS

Through the use of an attitude questionnaire, designed to ascertain the political orientations or attitudes of decision makers toward people, issues, and institutions, the author examined the hypothesis that there would be found a cohesive nationalism among a sample of the political elite drawn from the Illia administration. The sample comprises sixty-eight members of the political elite in the Illia administration and includes representatives of each of the three sectors (NES, Gubernatorial, Legislative).[3] Members of the following political parties participated: eight Progressive Democrats (PDP), three Autonomists, three from the Movement of Integration and Development (MID), three from the Union of the Argentine People, (UDELPA), sixteen from the People's Radical Civic Union (UCRP), five from the Intransigent Radical Civic Union (UCRI), eight from the Justicialist Party, three from the Christian Democrat Party (PDC), seven from the Federation of Center Parties (FPC), two from the Argentine Socialist Party (PSA), two from the Democratic Socialist Party (PSD), and one each from the Popular Party of Salta, Radical Civic Union, Confederation of Provincial Parties, Conservative Party of Chaco, and the Federal Democratic Movement of Salta. There were two independents and one gave no party affiliation.

The questionnaires were administered by scheduled interviews and by mail. It was stressed to the respondents that the questionnaire was intended to record first impressions and that it was not necessary to elaborate in their responses. The general reaction, especially with those interviewed, was reluctance to accept these ground rules. The respondents admitted they felt boxed in by the alternatives "always," "only in case of emergency," "never," and "no opinion," and several took the opportunity to elaborate on their viewpoints. Although identification by name was not solicited, there were some who of their own volition affixed their signatures and, in some cases, seals of office to the questionnaire. By way of comparison, the questionnaire was administered also to a group of seventy-five university students—a potential source of political elite in Argentina—and where appropriate their attitudes on the issues will be shown.

The questionnaire consisted of four main parts: the first was intended to ascertain the general party affiliation of the respondent in order to discern those political parties with similar or dissimilar opinions; the second and third were geared to tap reactions to certain nationalist-oriented opinion items having to do with the general problem of development and political modernization; the fourth was intended to ascertain preferences toward possible presidential personalities.

The questionaire as a whole strove to elicit reactions suggestive of a pattern of nationalism among those persons representing the governing body of the Argentine nation. Underlying its simple design is the assumption that there is a connection between attitude and the phenomenon of nationalism as operationally defined. It should also be pointed out that the questionnaire was structured to enlist in the research effort the participation of a specialized group who by nature tend to frown on the questionnaire as a tool for social research.

With nationalism as the common denominator, the present study proceeds to inquire into certain salient issues which to date remain unresolved, possibly because of lack of agreement in the attitudes of the political elite toward them or perhaps because of some other reason (psychological or philosophical) not subject to routine analysis.

Before turning to the findings themselves, it may be helpful to consider briefly the nature of the research questions relating to this endeavor in the area of political attitudes. (See appendix.) On the premise that development constitutes one of the major concerns of the political elite (and of the entire nation, for that matter), it was asked: Do the political elite view state control as an answer to the problem? Do the political elite prefer a system which encourages foreign and free enterprise in the polity? Also, what kind of development projects do elites give top priority?

Another set of important questions asked of the political elite were: Should institutional groups in the polity, such as the military, political parties, church, and labor, have a role in the political life of the country? In order to gain some insight into the so-called "rules of the game" in the polity, it was asked: Should support for certain constitutional norms such as freedom of speech, press, and political opposition be limited? Should force or violence be used for the overthrow of government?

In order to determine whether the political elites tend to be universalistic (taking a world-view) or particularistic (taking a parochial view) in their dealings with other nations or international organizations, the following questions were asked: Should the economic integration of Latin America be realized? Is cooperation in the inter-American system important for national prestige? Should monetary and moral support be given the United Nations? Where economic development is involved, is cooperation with all nations indispensable, regardless of political ideology? Should immigration laws discriminate in regard to nationality? All these research problems relate to the over-all task of approximating, to a certain degree, the extent to which the political system might be committed to the defense of democratic values both at home and abroad.

GENERAL OBSERVATIONS

Modernization Projects

As in other Latin American countries, the ideal of the political elite in Argentina is the implementation of a successful development policy which will rid the nation of its *subdesarrol-*

lado ("underdevelopment") complex and enhance its prestige both at home and abroad. As many policy makers will admit, there is a great deal of disagreement on economic development policy and there are a large number of development and social reform projects which should be undertaken.

The second part of the questionnaire inquires into the relative desirability of six kinds of projects as measured by the votes of the 68 respondents. Housing projects, as indicated below, were ranked first in priority by the sample "poll." Cattle, Argentina's "Number 1" export, and agricultural production ranked second in importance. The installation of industrial plants was considered third in terms of priority, with public works projects, education, and hospitals, following in order.

Development Projects in Order of Priority	Percentage of Votes Received
Housing projects	41.2
Cattle raising and agricultural production	26.5
Industrial plants, installation of	14.7
Public works projects	8.8
Education	5.9
Hospitals	2.9

The university students interviewed with the same questionnaire ranked these projects in the following order:

Development Projects in Order of Priority	Percentage of Votes Received
Housing projects	26.4
Industrial plants, installation of	25.3
Cattle raising and agricultural production	16.4
Public works projects	15.4
Hospitals	8.8
Education	7.7

Attitudes Toward Economic Development

Behind the immediate political troubles preoccupying the modernizing elites in Argentina today is the perennial problem of economic development. The events in Argentina since Perón constitute a series of economic crises which have gravely weakened the prospects for the realization of social and political advancement as envisaged in such arrangements as the Alliance for Progress. Notwithstanding vast sums of aid from the United States and international institutions, the basic economic indicators show a rising index in the cost of living, a high rate of unemployment, and a huge deficit in the national budget. Anti-inflationary programs have so far been weak and ineffectual, lacking the general political support prerequisite for successful stabilization policies. The economic antidote for inflation has been devaluation. In the Illia administration, for example, there were seven devaluations of the Argentine peso; three in 1964, three in 1965, and one in 1966; and the inflationary spiral continues in the Onganía administration. This recurring pattern of economic stagnation has dealt a serious blow to Argentine pride and nationalism.

According to the Argentine economist, Carlos García Martínez, the entire concept of modernization revolves around productivity and how best it can be achieved for the modernizing nation. It is also suggested that this ideal of productivity should imbue all social and economic structures of the polity, thus creating the necessary conditions for a smooth process of change from the old to the new.[4] Indeed, government controls have been found to vary in the Argentine context depending upon the nationalist bent of the political executive in charge of the ship of state. At times executives have found it necessary to attack foreign capitalism and free enterprise as a political expedient. In the interest of development, however, political decision-makers have been wont to exhibit an economic liberalism characterized by an admixture of isolationist and internationalist attitudes.[5]

The classic economic doctrine of capitalism predicated on a free economy with minimum interference by the state only serves to exacerbate the demands of a frustrated people for modernization through paternalistic action by the state. As a strategy for development, Arturo Frondizi's idea of "national programming" seems to offer a third choice in addition to what in Latin America may be considered the harsh disciplines of capitalism and collectivism. Frondizi's idea of national programming suggested that sustained national development could not be achieved except by establishing democracy in the Argentine political process. According to Frondizi, the total incorporation of the "popular majorities" into the democratic process would prove essential in the Argentine nation's struggle for economic development.[6] What Frondizi emphasized was free elections with no holds barred, the result of which, depending on the victor, would provide the authentic motor for economic change in the political system. It is problematical, however, whether Argentines would agree on Frondizi's strategy as a national idea.

Table VII indicates that more than 60 per cent of the political elite interviewed believe that public services and natural resources should be under government control, and 70 per cent believe that free enterprise and increased foreign investment are indispensable in the economic development of the country; however, approximately the same number do not want foreign enterprise or capital investment admitted into the country; nor do they believe that government intervention is desirable in regard to private enterprise.

By comparison, 49 per cent of the university students interviewed responded affirmatively to the proposition that public services and natural resources should be under government control. Sixty-three per cent favored free enterprise and increase in foreign investment to aid the economic development of the country. There were 44 per cent of the students (as compared to 78 per cent of the political elite) who agreed that foreign investment should not be admitted to the country, and 57 per cent indicated that government intervention is not desirable in regard to private enterprise.

TABLE VII
ATTITUDES TOWARD SPECIFIC ISSUES
RELATED TO ECONOMIC DEVELOPMENT

Propositions	Distribution ($n = 68$)		
	Opinion	No.	Per cent
Essential public services should be administrated through the state.	Always	42	61.8
	In emergency only	4	5.9
	Never	3	4.4
	Other *	9	13.2
	No opinion	10	14.7
Natural resources should be under government control.	Always	51	75.0
	In emergency only	10	14.7
	Never	5	7.4
	No opinion	2	2.9
Free enterprise and increase in foreign investment are indispensable to aid the economic development of the country.	Always	48	70.6
	In emergency only	6	8.8
	Never	6	8.8
	No opinion	8	11.8
Foreign enterprise or capital investment should not be admitted into the country.	Always	53	77.9
	In emergency only	12	17.7
	Never	3	4.4
	No opinion	—	—
Less government intervention is desirable in regard to private enterprise.	Always	48	70.6
	In emergency only	4	5.9
	Never	11	16.2
	No opinion	5	7.3

* Some believe that it depends on the norms of each country, others prefer public services provided by mixed or private enterprises with the control of the state.

Limitation of Basic Freedoms and Violence

As in matters relating to economic development, the political elite in Argentina demonstrate varying views on the "rules of the game" intended by the regime to provide some order and stability to the political process. The Argentine people are known

for the rugged character of their individualism which will tolerate little or no encroachment upon their civil privileges as members of the state. In defense of these privileges, the thesis is often
invoked that violence should be used for the displacement of
individuals, groups, and parties regarded as unfit to manage the
affairs of the polity. It is not unusual for violence to assume the
role of nationalism (i.e. the preservation of the nation) sometimes taking on the proportions of militarism (i.e. the exercise
of military control) or legalism (i.e. strict adherence to laws) in
the politics of a nation such as Argentina. Despite Argentina's
staggering record of coups and concurrent suspensions of basic
freedoms, there is little evidence to substantiate the institution-
alization of violence as a social value in the political life of the
country. It is very interesting to observe how political elites feel
about this phenomenon as shown in Table VIII.

In comparison to the political elite group, 70 per cent of the
university students responded to the first proposition that violence
should be used as a means of overthrowing the government only
in case of emergency. The majority of students also stated that
freedom of speech, press, and opposition should not be limited.

The Role of Institutional Groups

In describing the Argentine political crisis, the temptation is
ever present to accentuate the phenomenon of violence inherent
in the political system and to minimize the democratic activism
present in the politics of the country. It should be pointed out
that there is no aversion in Argentina to a constitutionalism of
republican and representative democracy, but, there is a pal-
pable fear of what may be labeled absolutist adventures which
could lead to a dictatorship like that of a Rosas or a Perón.
There is also an increasing awareness among the people that the
administrations of the res publica is no easy task which can be
handled by one person or group without the constructive participation of other dissimilar groups in the polity. In this respect, it is worth noting the attitudes of the political elite toward
the influence wielded by such important institutional groups as
the military, Catholic Church, and labor.

TABLE VIII
ATTITUDES TOWARD SPECIFIC ISSUES RELATED TO
FREEDOMS, VIOLENCE, AND INSTITUTIONAL ROLES

Propositions	Distribution ($n = 68$)		
	Opinion	No.	Per cent
Violent means should be used to overthrow governments.	Always	1	1.5
	In emergency only	18	26.5
	Never	46	67.6
	No opinion	3	4.4
Freedom of speech, press, and political opposition should be limited.	Always	3	4.4
	In emergency only	23	33.8
	Never	42	61.8
	No opinion	—	—
The military should play an important role in the political life of the country.	Always	18	26.5
	In emergency only	26	38.2
	Never	23	33.8
	No opinion	1	1.5
The Catholic Church should play an important role in the political life of the country.	Always	29	42.7
	In emergency only	11	16.1
	Never	26	38.2
	No opinion	—	—
Labor unions should play an important role in the political life of the country.	Always	40	58.8
	In emergency only	6	8.9
	Never	22	32.3
	No opinion	—	—
Political parties should unite to support the government despite ideological differences.	Always	32	47.1
	In emergency only	22	32.3
	Never	—	—
	Other	10	14.7
	No opinion	4	5.8

The political elite were completely divided in their answers as to whether "the military should play an important role in the political life of the country." Table VIII shows the even distribution of answers among "always," "only in an emergency," and "never."

Among the university students, 50 per cent stated that the military should play an important role in the country in cases of emergency; 45 per cent stated that the Catholic Church should always play an important role in the polity; and 67 per cent believed that labor unions should also play a part in the political life of the country.

Political Parties and Ideological Differences

During the author's visit to Argentina shortly before the coup of 1966, it was possible to detect in conversations with different political leaders in diverse and sometimes opposing parties what might be described as a general spirit of compromise among the elites, and beyond that, a willingness on their part to meet with each other and to work out differences with ballots rather than bullets. In light of this observation the responses of the political elite to the item in the questionnaire relating to the possibility of compromise regardless of ideological differences are especially noteworthy.

On the whole, the political elite queried would seem to consider the support of the government more important than personal or political ideological differences. It is noted that almost 15 per cent of the respondents considered this issue important enough to *ad lib* rather than just answer with an "X." [7]

Views on Internationalism

As a political system evolves, the various agencies of political socialization strive to instill certain nationalist attitudes in the citizen which will enable him to champion the nation's cause both at home and abroad. Where the phenomenon of nationalism is involved, it can be argued that no country lends itself to more difficult analysis than Argentina, which abounds with "nationalisms." Where the Argentines and the rest of Latin America are concerned, it is in order to relate nationalism to internationalism, for it can be said of Latin American countries that their nationalism shades off into internationalism.[8]

In considering the internationalist aspect of Argentine nationalism the importance of Argentina as one of the three major powers in Latin America should be stressed. It is known that the country plays a key role in the process of economic development of the region as stimulated by the Latin America common market. But, in view of the unpredictable character of her nationalism, it is difficult to predict to what extent full cooperation will be attained in this effort.

In the area of inter-American collaboration, Argentine nationalism has been known to be obstructionist and remarkably eclectic in its general orientation toward such principles as nonintervention, continentalism, self-determination, and sovereignty. Where the United States is concerned, Argentine nationalism has tended to be xenophobic and protectionist in character, leaving little room for any overly optimistic expectations on the part of the United States and other countries of the West in regard to the prospects for bargaining out differences on a basis of reciprocity within a general framework of common interests. As we examine the internationalist attitudes of the Argentine policy-making elites, it is important to remember that these attitudes are shaped by the socializing influences of the political community.

Table IX indicates that the political elite in our sample consider the economic integration of Latin America and cooperation in the inter-American system important for Argentina. It is also interesting to note that the university students responded favorably to these quesions. Seventy-seven per cent stated that economic integration of Latin America is necessary, and 85 per cent admitted that cooperation in the inter-American system is important for national prestige.

It would seem also that cooperation with all nations, regardless of political ideology, is important to the decision-making elite in Argentina where economic development is involved. And this group responded to the question regarding monetary and moral support for the United Nations with an overwhelming affirmative. The same enthusiasm was noted among the university students, with 83 per cent of the respondents expressing agreement with the proposition.

time the prominent man of the party machine. At times, however, outstanding national figures have headed party lists, presented by an important dissident *caudillo* but without the support of the party machine. Those *caudillos* who have their way within the party (the *caudillos máximos* of the party) are able to make absolute decisions regarding the choice of presidential candidate. The selection of a candidate is normally made from among the presidential possibilities of the party. The person selected immediately becomes a captive of the group of *caudillos* who sponsored him, which, as in other countries, results in his doling out political plums after election.

When confronted with the responsibility of making a political choice of candidate for the presidency of the nation, it would seem reasonable to assume that the political elite would give their vote to the outstanding figure representing their party. It may be, however, that given a second choice, they may opt for other prominent figures for this office, whether from within or outside of their party. The following rank order of political leaders selected by respondents to the questionnaire for the office of President underscores this point. For example, Horacio Thedy, a leader of the Progressive Democrat Party, received eight votes for first choice; eight questionnaires were answered by the Progressive Democrat Party. Juan Perón, represented by the Justicialist Party, came in second in this category with seven votes; there were eight respondents from the Justicialist Party. Eleven of the 16 respondents from the UCRP split their votes between Balbín and Illia. This first-choice category seems to substantiate the partisan loyalty of the political elite, their unwillingness to cross party lines. The second-choice category reveals the names of Juan Onganía, a military man without party affiliation, Raúl Matera of the Justicialist Party, and Julio Cueto Rúa of the Argentine Republican Party (PRAR). Here, party loyalties tend to be side-stepped and individual opinions prevail, favoring candidates having no connection with the individual's party. None of the first three persons named in the second-choice category held public office at the time the questionnaire was administered. Interestingly enough, the university students made Arturo Fron-

TABLE X
RANK ORDER OF POLITICAL LEADERS FOR OFFICE
OF PRESIDENT AS SELECTED BY RESPONDENTS

First Choice	Political Party	No. of Votes Recv'd.	Second Choice	Political Party	No. of Votes Recv'd.
Thedy	PDP	8	Onganía	Military	7
Perón	Justicialist	7	Matera	Justicialist	4
Illia	UCRP	6	Cueto Rúa	PRAR	3
Alende	UCRI	5	Balbín	UCRP	3
Balbín	UCRP	5	Illia	UCRP	3
Jofre	FPC	4	Aramburu	UDELPA	2
Frondizi	MID	4			
Aramburu	UDELPA	3			
Total *		42	Total **		24
(n = 68, 21 did not answer)			(n = 68, 33 did not answer)		

* One vote was given to each of the following: Onganía (Military), Ocampo, Lozano, Soria, and Martijeno (party affiliations unknown).
** One vote was given to each of the following: Alende (UCRI), Perette (UCRP), Frondizi (MID), Alfonsin, Pastorino, Sueldo, Marina, Aznar, Rotundo, Solano Lima (party affiliations unknown), and Zavala Ortiz (UCRP).

dizi first choice for President, with Onganía receiving second choice, as shown by Table XI.

The author readily states that a definite conclusion cannot be reached from such a small sampling of the political elite. The above data should be considered nothing more than tentative indications of what party affiliates might do if given an alternative.

A tally of each candidate's total votes was made to see how individuals compared. Each time a candidate's name was chosen for an office, whether for first or second choice, he received one vote. According to this criterion, the following were given the most votes for President by the sample of political elite.

First place: Illia, Balbín (tie)
Second place: Thedy, Onganía (tie)

TABLE XI
RANK ORDER OF POLITICAL LEADERS FOR OFFICE
OF PRESIDENT AS SELECTED BY UNIVERSITY STUDENTS

First Choice	Political Party	No. of Votes Recv'd.	Second Choice	Political Party	No. of Votes Recv'd.
Frondizi	MID	11	Onganía	Military	6
Cueto Rúa	PRAR	6	Aramburu	UDELPA	4
Onganía	Military	5	Frondizi	MID	3
Aramburu	UDELPA	4	Matera	Justicialist	3
Sueldo	PDC	3	Sueldo	PDC	3
Alsogaray	Military	3	Thedy	PDP	3
Illia	UCRP	2	Alsogaray	Military	2
Balbín	UCRP	2	Alende	UCRI	2
Rauch	Unknown	2	Begnis	Unknown	2
			Illia	UCRP	2
			Zavala O.	UCRP	2
Total *		40	Total **		32
(n = 75, 30 did not answer)			(n = 75, 40 did not answer)		

* One vote was given to each of the following: Perón (Just.), Bengoa (Military), Matera (Just.), Guevara, Ferrer (Party affiliations unknown).
** One vote was given to each of the following: Jofre (FPC), Perón (Just.), Rauch (party affiliation unknown).

The following result was shown for the same office as selected by the group of university students.

First place: Onganía

Second place: Frondizi

It might be useful to give something of the background of a few of the political leaders who were considered by the political elite as well as by the universitarians questioned to be their choice to lead the nation.

Alvaro Alsogaray is a civil and military engineer, born in Esperanza, province of Sante Fe, in 1913. He was President of Argentina's Merchant Air Fleet in 1950, subsecretary of Ministry of Economy in 1955, and Minister of Industries in 1956. He was

Minister of Economy from 1959 to 1961 and held several other appointive posts during the Frondizi and Guido governments. Pedro Aramburu is a retired army general. He was provisional president of Argentina from 1955 to 1958. He is a strong opponent of Perón but believes Peronists should be reintegrated into political life of the nation. He is a member of the Union of the Argentine People (UDELPA), a party formed to promote his candidacy in 1963.

Ricardo Balbín was born in Buenos Aires in 1904. He received a degree in law in 1926 from the Faculty of Law and Social Sciences at the University of La Plata. He served two terms as national deputy from the province of Buenos Aires (1946–1948 and 1948–1949); was a candidate for the Presidency of the Nation for the *Union Cívica Radical* in 1951; and in the elections of 1958 for the *Partido Unión Cívica Radical del Pueblo* (UCRP).

Julio Cueto Rúa is a university professor and lawyer by profession. He was born in La Plata, Buenos Aires province, in 1920. He received a fellowship from Southern Methodist University School of Law in Dallas, where he received the Master of Laws in Comparative Law with the distinction of summa cum laude. He is director of "Consultores Asociados."

Arturo Frondizi, who was born in Paso de los Libres, Corrientes province, in 1908, was president of Argentina from May 1958 to March 1962. He is a lawyer, editor, writer, and politician. He was national deputy from 1946 to 1952, was Balbín's vice presidential running mate against the Perón-Quijano ticket in 1951, and in 1957 led the UCRI faction out of the old UCR party in the split to promote his own presidential candidacy.

Arturo Illia is a physician, born in the city of Pergamino, Buenos Aires province, in 1900. He was provincial senator in Córdoba from 1936–1940; national deputy from Córdoba, 1948–1952; and president of the Argentine Republic from 1963 to June, 1966, when a military coup replaced his administration with General Juan Carlos Onganía.

Raúl Matera is an internationally known neurosurgeon, born in Buenos Aires in 1915. He has written several works in his profession and was subdirector of the Institute of Neurosurgery of the Faculty of Medical Sciences of Buenos Aires. He has a political reputation for moderate views within the Peronist movement.

Juan Carlos Onganía was born in Marcos Paz, Buenos Aires province, in 1914, and graduated from the Military College of the Nation in 1934. He was Commander in Chief of the Army during the Illia administration. In November 1965, upon the designation by Illia of General Castro Sánchez as Secretary of War, General Onganía asked to be relieved of his post, and was succeeded by General Pascual A. Pistarini. After the successful coup of June 1966, he became President of Argentina.

Carlos H. Perette was born in Paraná, province of Entre Ríos, in 1915. He is a lawyer and has been provincial and national deputy for the province of Santa Fe, and Vice President of the Nation from 1963 to 1966.

Juan Domingo Perón, former President of Argentina, has been in exile since 1955 and at present directs the Peronist movement from Spain. He was a member of the United Officers' Group (G.O.U.) which was instrumental in the 1943 revolution. He was Secretary of Labor and Social Welfare, Minister of War, and Vice President from 1943 to 1945. He was President of Argentina from 1946 to 1955, when he was deposed by military *coup d'état*.

Horacio J. Sueldo is a lawyer and university professor. He was born in Villa del Rosario, province of Córdoba, in 1923. He was vice presidential candidate for the Christian Democrat Party in 1958 and presidential candidate for this same party in 1963.

Horacio Ricardo Thedy was born in Rosario, province of Sante Fe, in 1906. He is a lawyer and university professor. Sr. Thedy was Pedro Aramburu's running mate for the Progressive Democrat Party and the Union of the Argentine People Party in the 1963 elections. He has written several books in his profession and was national deputy from 1963 to 1966.

Miguel Zavala Ortiz is a Doctor of Jurisprudence and Professor of Commercial Law in the Faculty of Law and Social Sciences at the University of Buenos Aires. He was national deputy from Córdoba from 1949 to 1953. Dr. Zavala Ortiz was a strong contender in the UCRP for presidential nomination in 1958, but lost to Balbín.

A CONCLUDING NOTE

The general assumption of this pioneer experiment is that attitude and the phenomenon of nationalism are related. We cannot conclude from our tentative findings that a marked degree of cohesive nationalism exists among the political elite who have been examined in this chapter in regard to the similarity of their reactions toward such issues as the selection of the presidential candidate, consensus on modernization projects, and the relative participation of such institutional groups as the military and church in the polity. Where questions involving party loyalty are concerned, such as deciding upon a candidate for the office of the national presidency, the political elite have tended to avoid decisions which may conflict with the value system of the party they represent. There is some evidence that does point to a relative cohesiveness of the elite in matters relating to the preservation of civil rights and interparty cooperation in the political system. The latter is interesting when one considers the endemic immobilism which plagues the Argentine system.

A broad spectrum of political parties which reflect different ideologies constitutes the Argentine political network. The possibility of interparty cooperation would seem to have bearing on whether a government may emerge from such a matrix of parties with the strength and disposition to sacrifice those local interests for an international effort on the scale of the Alliance for Progress or Latin-American Free Trade Association. The nationalist feelings among the political elite also seem to reflect consensus regarding the feasibility of Latin American economic integration. In the sphere of international politics, however, the political elite indicated a low tolerance for interventionist policies even where human rights and democratic principles are being abused. For many leaders the principle of national self-determination remains a political imperative in Argentine foreign policy. It is noted that among the elite examined there was a general agreement in support of the inter-American system and the United Nations.

In terms of what the data reveal, Argentine elite attitudes examined do not tend to conform to one variety or pattern. They reflect instead a rich diversity and diffuseness characteristic of a political culture which is still in the process of development.

NOTES

1. Eisenstadt, *Essays on Sociological Aspects of Political and Economic Development*, p. 39.

2. See Fernández, "The Nationalism Syndrome in Argentina," pp. 563–564.

3. The sample actually employed was a nonrandom group comprising those political elite who cooperated by answering the attitude questionnaire (see Appendix). Thus, the observations made are tentative and not intended to characterize the political attitudes of the Illia administration.

4. Martínez, *La Inflación Argentina*, pp. 375–376.

5. See Thomas F. McGann, *Argentina: The Divided Land*, pp. 74–75.

6. See Arturo Frondizi, *Estrategia y Táctica del Movimiento Nacional, passim;* see also Frondizi, *La Alianza para el Progreso*, p. 46.

7. Typical responses read as follows:

"If they are democratic governments respectful of liberty, then political parties should unite."

"Circumstantially, yes, to maintain the stability of the constitutional government."

"When formulating a plan of agreement."

"Depends on the government."

"Stability is convenient and necessary and the agreements of parties ought to be a medium of assurance in case of national emergency."

8. Arthur P. Whitaker and David C. Jordan, *Nationalism in Contemporary Latin America*, pp. 6–7.

CHAPTER 7

REFLECTIONS ON
THE POLITICAL ELITE
IN ARGENTINA

In this book the Argentine polity has been considered basically in terms of the operation of various important groups such as the military, church, labor, business, university, and party which, as agents of political socialization, influence the milieu in which the elites operate.

The expression of interests among these divergent groups is nationalist and modern, if not reformist, in its orientation to the goals of development. It can be said that the process of political selection takes place in a modernizing culture wherein the party is the main agent. Recruitment by the multiple parties in the political system is characterized by formality and personalism. *Caudillismo* pervades the selection process and is still very much alive in Argentine politics. Sometimes the *caudillo* appears as a self-appointed candidate for political office. There are occasions, however, when he may simply wish to work as an *hombre de votos*. He may prefer to manipulate political aspirants by garnering votes, in the intraparty selection process, using them in favor of the person he selects to run for a particular post. This *caudillistic* pattern which inheres in political relationships is indicative of a condition best described as something less than accelerative development.

Whether by deliberate design of political leaders or not, the achievement of political maturity has been stymied in Argentina. There is no doubt that the political system is in the process of evolution toward workable institutions and practices but, as one observer put it to the author, *le falta madurez*. In other words, maturity is lacking in the system. This situation, of course, cannot be blamed on the citizenry. One might perhaps prefer to blame a peculiar set of circumstances which the Argentine often labels *la fatalidad*, "fate." The Argentine people are sometimes compared to a *niño mimado*, or "spoiled child," who has always enjoyed the best of everything. Collectively, the country has never lacked natural or intellectual resources. It has never suffered the sting of a major war, quite on the contrary, war has favored the economy. This *niño-mimado* concept suggests an important theoretical point of departure for analysis of the political retardation evidenced in the Argentine syndrome of development. Reluctance on the part of the Argentine rulers and ruled to conform to any established pattern of authority and consent attests the erratic character of the country which does not correspond to any other type of political government in Latin America.

In developing societies, the capacity to modernize is intimately related to political leadership. The political leadership, for example, is expected to be competent and capable of regulating the multidimensional process of social change in the direction of appropriate societal goals. This is indeed a large order requiring a politically efficient and informed leadership and a wide margin of error for the governing elite responsible for making acceptable choices in matters of public policy.

If educational achievement is a measure of political competence, Argentina has a great deal of which to be proud. As the data in Chapter 5 reveal, the majority of those persons occupying important political office have obtained a substantial degree of education which would seem to equip them for the stability and progress in the direction of nation-building. As in other developing and even developed countries, the majority of the political leaders are drawn from the legal profession and are relatively young and yet experienced persons. Those who have attained important posts in the decision-making apparatus have in the main demonstrated a high political-activity index. What this means in terms of competence and experience is that the average Argentine leader is a seasoned, politicized individual.

It is very unusual for a nonpolitical person to occupy an important governmental post. High-prestige political positions tend to remain in the province of those who have displayed top-level performance in the rugged *cursus honorum* to the satisfaction of either a *Comité* or *Caudillo*. It should be pointed out that in democratically organized parties in contrast to vertically structured ones it is necessary for aspiring leaders seeking to move up the political ladder to subject themselves to the most rigorous discipline and training in the study and the handling of public problems and issues. As has been indicated earlier, the political mobility of the elite, in the sense of circulation from one elective post to the next, has tended to be relatively high, thus contributing to their political seasoning and experience.

The influence of *peronismo* in the stratum of political leadership has not diminished despite the divisionism and contradictory tendencies which exist within the movement. It was noted that the working (peronist) class made noticeable gains in the ranks of the political elite. Under the Justicialist banner a significant number of the middle class—professionals and merchants—qualified for and won entry into elite positions. These individuals were for the most part a young and energetic group of syndicalist origin, some of whom had attended institutions of higher education. Their emergence in top leadership posts was in great part owing to the climate of coexistence which Frondizi had cultivated in 1958 and which Illia sought to perpetuate to the dissatisfaction of the military sector.

In view of the high level of urbanization in the Argentine republic, it would seem difficult for democratic leadership, in the sense of representativeness in political elite positions, to be achieved in the recruitment process. National growth in Argentina has been characterized by what is sometimes referred to as macrocephalic development with considerable demographic displacement from the interior into the port area. The data examined do not reveal to what degree the unitary character of Argentine federalism affects the recruitment process, nor whether any relationship exists between these two variables.

What the data show, however, is that a relatively proportionate representation characterizes the composition of the political leadership. Not only are the political elite recruited from a broad professional base, but they are also characterized by considerable heterogeneity of geographic origins.

In political systems, democratic development is contingent upon the effectiveness of socialization efforts toward the acceptance of democratic norms and practices. Argentina takes pride in its rich heritage of democratic values. Each political regime in the coup-ridden experience of this country has sought in its own way to mold and institutionalize these values into a workable national system. The question one immediately asks is why so many regimes have failed. Is it because Argentine political leaders are essentially antidemocratic in their attitudes toward policy decisions? As was noted in Chapter 6, those political elite who answered the attitude questionnaire intimated general support for the ideas of democracy, political organization, self-determination, aversion to violence as a political means, and the desirability of progress, as well as economic development through regional integration and peace through international cooperation.

It has been stressed that the idea of modernization as a social value has gained wide acceptance in the Argentine polity. However, the political consensus required to make this idea of modernization a reality is still lacking in the system. General commitment on the part of the political elites to democratic norms would seem to contribute little in an atmosphere where elite patterns of interaction in the power structure fail to create legitimacy and stability for the system. The crisis of leadership in

Argentina is one of legitimacy and instability—a crisis which can be surmounted only to the extent that interaction among the political elite and other elite groups (military, church, labor, business) is conducive to citizens' identification with and political participation in a culture of shared interests.

What is being suggested here is that in addition to the idea of modernization, the idea of national community must imbue the political system. The search for stable and effective political solutions for the endemic instability in the modernizing system continues. In the quest for a panacea, there is general support for the idea of structural change to embody the participation of all important elite groups performing specialized roles in the national interest. One study makes the following recommendations: that the middle class become politically participant with a modern outlook in conjunction with the masses; that political parties adapt their leadership to the demands of modernization; that the agrarian sector conform to the change process providing for the equitable distribution of land for maximum productivity; that business work hand in hand with labor even to the point of sharing the responsibility of management with the latter; that the armed forces, not unlike the church and other cultural institutions, demonstrate awareness of this critical responsibility in the modernization process; that labor as an organized unit provide the necessary leadership (political and ideological) to spearhead the process of change.[1]

In an atmosphere of distrust and impatience with constitutionally elected authority, it will be difficult to implement these and other national objectives. To the extent that a constitutional political elite in Argentina has failed to carry out nation-building responsibilities, the reason has not been because of improper political attitudes or marginal quality of the leadership. What must be pointed out is that it has been difficult for a decision-making elite to perform a political function satisfactorily in a milieu of recurring military interference and discontinuance of elected regimes. It would seem that the principle of fair play would not allow a constitutional leadership to be judged incompetent before it is permitted to serve its term.

As the situation now presents itself in Argentina, we may hypothesize that from the standpoint of political development and stability, a workable system of interaction can be developed among the dissident groups of the politically articulate strata only to the extent that a basis of confidence between political and military leaders is established.

NOTES

1. "La CGT y el cambio de estructuras," pp. 9–11.

APPENDIX

CUESTIONARIO

1. Los siguientes son algunos de los partidos políticos en el sistema político argentino:

Federación de Partidos de Centro (FPC)

Frente Nacional y Popular (FNP)

Justicialista (J)

Movimiento de Integración y Desarrollo (MID)

Partido Comunista Argentino (PCA)

Partido Demócrata Cristiano (PDC)

Partido Demócrata Progresista (PDP)

Partido Republicano de la Argentina (PRAR)

Partido Socialista Argentino (PSA)

Partido Socialista Democrático (PSD)

Unión Cívica Radical del Pueblo (UCRP)

Unión Cívica Radical Intransigente (UCRI)

Unión Conservadora (UC)

Unión del Pueblo Argentino (UDELPA)

Unión Popular (UP)

111

De dichos partidos, sírvase indicar:
a. A cuál está usted afiliado ....
b. Si no está usted afiliado en ninguno de ellos, sírvase mencionar a qué otro está afiliado ....
c. Cuál(es) de dichos partidos tiene(n) opiniones parecidas a las suyas ....
d. Cuál(es) de dichos partidos tiene(n) opiniones distintas a las suyas ....
e. Si no opina sobre estas preguntas sírvase marcar una "X" en el siguiente espacio ....

2. Sírvase clasificar en lista de prioridad lo siguiente. Por ejemplo:

Proyectos de viviendas	1 (Primero)
Proyectos de hospital	2 (Segundo)

a. Proyectos de aumentar productos agrícolas y ganaderos. ....
b. Proyectos de instalar plantas industriales. ....
c. Proyectos de obras públicas. ....
d. Proyectos de viviendas. ....
e. Proyectos de hospitales. ....
f. Otro ....

3. Sírvase indicar cómo decidiría usted en las siguientes instancias.

	Siempre	Sólo en caso de emergencia nacional	Nunca	No tengo Opinión
a. No deberían ser admitidas en el país las empresas extranjeras o inversiones de capital extranjero.				

	Siempre	Sólo en caso de emergencia nacional	Nunca	No tengo Opinión
b. Deben ser limitadas la libertad de palabra, de prensa y de oposición política.	....	....	....	....
c. El plan de obras públicas debe acentuar el desarrollo económico y la necesidad de mejorar el nivel de vida.	....	....	....	....
d. Los recursos naturales deben estar bajo el control del gobierno.	....	....	....	....
e. Los militares deben desempeñar una parte importante en la vida política del país.	....	....	....	....
f. Debe realizarse la integración económica de América Latina.	....	....	....	....
g. La libre empresa y el aumento de la inversión extranjera son indispensables para asistir al desarrollo económico del país.	....	....	....	....
h. Es importante para el prestigio nacional la cooperación en el sistema interamericano.	....	....	....	....
i. La Iglesia católica debe desempeñar una				

	Siempre	Sólo en caso de emergencia nacional	Nunca	No tengo Opinión
parte importante en la vida política del país.	....	....	....	....
j. Cuando se trata del desarrollo económico, es indispensable la cooperación con todas las naciones, sean cuales fueren las ideologías políticas.	....	....	....	....
k. Deben utilizarse medios violentos para derribar al gobierno.	....	....	....	....
l. Los partidos políticos deben unirse para mantener al gobierno a pesar de las diferencias ideológicas.	....	....	....	....
m. Los sindicatos obreros deben desempeñar una parte importante en la vida política del país.	....	....	....	....
n. Las leyes de inmigración deben discriminar en cuanto a nacionalidad.	....	....	....	....
o. Es deseable tener menos intervención del gobierno en cuanto a las empresas privadas.	....	....	....	....
p. Debe darse apoyo monetario y moral a				

las Naciones Unidas
como una Organi-
zación internacional
para la preservación
de la paz.

q. Los servicios públicos
esenciales deben ad-
ministrarse a través
del Estado, o admite
alguna forma de inter-
vención privada, sea
nacional o extranjera.

r. Cuando los derechos
humanos y las institu-
ciones democráticas
están amenazadas en
un país, corresponde
la intervención for-
ánea en los asuntos de
dicho país.

4. Sírvase ordenar según las categorías de primera, segunda y
tercera su selección para el puesto de Presidente o Vicepresidente de la República Argentina:

Julio Cueto Rúa   Horacio Sueldo
Oscar Alende   José María Guido
Alvaro Alsogaray   Arturo Illia
Pedro Aramburu   Raúl Matera
Ricardo Balbín   Juan C. Onganía
León Justo Bengoa   Juan Domingo Perón
Andrés Framini   Enrique Rauch
Arturo Frondizi   Miguel A. Zavala Ortiz
Emilio Jofré   Vicente Solano Lima

Horacio Thedy   Carlos H. Perette
Augusto Vandor
                          Otro: ....
a. Presidente: ....
                          Primera   Segunda   Tercera
b. Vicepresidente: ....
                          Primera   Segunda   Tercera

QUESTIONNAIRE

1. The following are some of the political parties in the Argentine political system:

Federation of Center Parties   Argentine Socialist Party
(FPC)   (PSA)

Popular National Front   Democratic Socialist Party
(FNP)   (PSD)

Justicialist (J)   People's Radical Civic Union
                                    (UCRP)

Movement of Integration and   Intransigent Radical Civic
Development (MID)   Union (UCRI)

Argentine Communist Party   Conservative Union (UC)
(PCA)

Christian Democrat Party   Union of the Argentine
(PDC)   People (UDELPA)

Progressive Democrat Party   Popular Union Party (UP)
(PDP)

Argentine Republican Party
(PRAR)

From said parties, please indicate:
a. With which are you affiliated ....
b. If you are not affiliated with any of them, please mention
    with which other one you are affiliated ....

    ....

c. Which of said parties holds opinions similar to yours

    ....

d. Which of said parties has opinions different from yours

e. If you have no opinion regarding these questions please mark an "X" in the following space ....

2. Please list according to priority the following. For example:
   Hospital projects   1 (First)
   Housing projects   2 (Second)
   a. Projects of cattle raising and
      Agricultural production.   ....
   b. Projects of installing industrial
      plants.   ....
   c. Public works projects.   ....
   d. Housing projects.   ....
   e. Hospital projects.   ....
   f. Other ....

3. Please indicate how you would decide in the following instances:

	Always	Only in case of National emergency	Never	No Opinion
a. Foreign enterprise or investment should not be admitted into the country.	....	....	....	....
b. Freedom of speech, press, and political opposition should be limited.	....	....	....	....
c. Public works projects should emphasize economic development and the need for improving the standard of living.	....	....	....	....

	Always	Only in case of National emergency	Never	No Opinion
d. Natural resources should be under government control.	....	....	....	....
e. The military should play an important role in the political life of the country.	....	....	....	....
f. The economic integragration of Latin Amershould be realized.	....	....	....	....
g. Free enterprise and foreign investment are indispensable to aid the economic development of the country.	....	....	....	....
h. Cooperation in the inter-American system is important for national prestige.	....	....	....	....
i. The Catholic Church should play an important role in the political life of the country.	....	....	....	....
j. Where economic development is involved, cooperation with all nations is indispensable, regardless of political ideology.	....	....	....	....
k. Violent means should be used to overthrow governments.	....	....	....	....

	Always	Only in case of National emergency	Never	No Opinion
l. Political parties should unite to support the government despite ideological differences.	....	....	....	....
m. Labor unions should play an important role in the political life of the country.	....	....	....	....
n. Immigration laws should discriminate in regard to nationality.	....	....	....	....
o. Government intervention is desirable in regard to private enterprise.	....	....	....	....
p. Monetary and moral support should be given the United Nations as an international organization for the preservation of peace.	....	....	....	....
q. Essential public services should be administered through the state.	....	....	....	....
r. When human rights and democratic institutions are threatened in a country, foreign intervention in the affairs of said country is permitted.	....	....	....	....

4. Please order according to the categories of first, second, and third your selection for the post of president or vice-president of the Argentine Republic:

Julio Cueto Rúa	Horacio Sueldo
Oscar Alende	José María Guido
Alvaro Alsogaray	Arturo Illia
Pedro Aramburu	Raúl Matera
Ricardo Balbín	Juan C. Onganía
León Justo Bengoa	Juan D. Perón
Andrés Framini	Enrique Rauch
Arturo Frondizi	Miguel A. Zavala Ortiz
Emilio Jofré	Vicente Solano Lima
Horacio Thedy	Carlos H. Perette
Augusto Vandor	

Other   ....

a. President   ....

                  First   Second   Third

b. Vice-president: ....

                  First   Second   Third

BIBLIOGRAPHY

A. BOOKS

Adúriz, Joaquín, S. J., "Religión," in Paita, ed., *Argentina, 1930–1960*. Buenos Aires: Editorial SUR S.R.L., 1961.

Agger, Robert A., Daniel Goldrich, and Bert E. Swanson, *The Rulers and the Ruled—Political Power and Impotence in American Communities*. New York: John Wiley & Sons, Inc., 1964.

Alexander, Robert J., *Communism in Latin America*. New Brunswick, N.J.: Rutgers University Press, 1957.

Almond, Gabriel A., "Introduction: A Functional Approach to Comparative Politics," in Gabriel A. Almond and James S. Coleman, eds., *The Politics of the Developing Areas*, Princeton, N.J.: Princeton University Press, 1960.

——— and Sidney Verba, *The Civic Culture*, Princeton, N.J.: Princeton University Press, 1963.

Apter, David E., *The Politics of Modernization*. Chicago: University of Chicago Press, 1967.

Barager, Joseph R., ed., *Why Perón Came to Power*. New York: Alfred A. Knopf, 1968.

Beck, Carl, James M. Malloy, and William R. Campbell, *A Survey of Elite Studies*. Washington, D.C.: Special Operations Research Office, American University, 1965.

Bell, Wendell, *Jamaican Leaders: Political Attitudes in a New Nation*. Berkeley: University of California Press, 1964.

Beyhaut, Gustavo, *et al.*, "Los Inmigrantes en el Sistema Occupacional Argentina," in Torcuato S. DiTella, Gino Germani, Jorge Graciarena, y colaboradores, eds., *Argentina, Sociedad de Masas*, Buenos Aires: Editorial Universitaria de Buenos Aires, 1965.

Bianchin, Orlando, *Qué Hacer Con los Partidos Políticos?* Buenos Aires: Editorial Campos S. En C. por A., 1965.

Bidart Campos, Germán J., *Grupos de Presión y Factores de Poder*. Buenos Aires: A. Peña Lillo, 1961.

Blanksten, George I., *Perón's Argentina*. Chicago: The University of Chicago Press, 1953.

————. "The Politics of Latin America," in Gabriel A. Almond and James S. Coleman, eds., *The Politics of the Developing Areas*, Princeton, N.J.: Princeton University Press, 1960.

Boletín Oficial de la República Argentina. Buenos Aires: Dirección Nacional del Registro Oficial, July 8, 1966.

Bottomore, T. B., *Elites and Society*. New York: Basic Books, Inc., 1964.

Campobassi, José S., *et al.*, *Los Partidos Políticos, Estructura y Vigencia en la Argentina*. Buenos Aires: Cooperadora de Derecho y Ciencias Sociales, 1963.

Carlevari, Isidro J. F., *La Argentina*. 2d ed. Buenos Aires: Editorial Ergon, 1964.

Castagno, Antonio, *Los Partidos Políticos Argentinos*. Buenos Aires: Roque Depalma, Editor, 1959.

Centro de Investigación y Acción Social, *Constituciones Provinciales Argentinas*, Tomo I. Buenos Aires: Del Atlántico, S.A., 1964.

Cline, Howard F., *Mexico: Revolution to Evolution, 1940–1960*. London: Oxford University Press, 1962.

Constitución Justicialista. Buenos Aires: Subsecretaría de Informaciones, 1954.

Cortés Conde, Roberto, "Partidos Políticos," in Paita, ed., *Argentina, 1930–1960*. Buenos Aires: Editorial SUR, S.R.L., 1961.

Cúneo, Dardo, *Informes*. Buenos Aires: Editorial Jorge Alvarez, S.A., 1966.

de Imaz, José Luis, *Los Que Mandan*. Buenos Aires: Editorial Universitaria de Buenos Aires, 1965.

del Mazo, Gabriel, *El Radicalismo: El Movimiento de Intransigencia y Renovación, 1945–1957*. Buenos Aires: Ediciones Gure, 1957.

————, *El Radicalismo: Notas Sobre su Historia y Doctrina, 1922–1952*. Buenos Aires: Ediciones Gure, 1959.

Ebenstein, William, *Great Political Thinkers, Plato to the Present*. New York: Holt, Rinehart and Winston, Inc., 1963.

Eisenstadt, S. N., *Essays on Sociological Aspects of Political and Economic Development*. The Hague, Netherlands: Mouton and Company, 1961.

Fayt, Carlos S., "La Organización Interna de los Partidos y los Métodos Políticos en la Argentina," in José S. Campobassi, *et al.*, eds., *Los Partidos Políticos, Estructura y Vigencia en la Argentina*. Buenos Aires: Cooperadora de Derecho y Ciencias Sociales, 1963.

Federación Nacional de Partidos de Centro, *Soluciones Conservadoras, 1962*. Buenos Aires: Unión Conservadora de la Provincia de Buenos Aires, 1962.

Fernández, Julio A., *Political Administration in Mexico*. Boulder: Bureau of Governmental Research, University of Colorado, 1969.

Fillol, Tomás Roberto, *Social Factors in Economic Development: The Argentine Case*. Cambridge, Mass.: Massachusetts Institute of Technology Press, 1961.

Frondizi, Arturo, *Estrategia y Táctica del Movimiento Nacional*. Buenos Aires: Editorial Desarrollo.

———, *La Alianza para el Progreso*. Buenos Aires: Editorial Desarrollo.

———, *Mensaje de Pacificación y Desarrollo Nacional*. Read before the Legislative Assembly by the President of the Nation, Dr. Arturo Frondizi, on the inauguration of his constitutional period. Buenos Aires: May 1, 1958.

Galletti, Alfredo, *La Realidad Argentina en el Siglo XX, La Política y los Partidos*, Tomo I. Buenos Aires: Fondo de Cultura Económica, 1961.

Ghioldi, Américo, *Juan B. Justo*. Buenos Aires: Ediciones Monserrat, 1964.

Grondona, Mariano, *Factores de Poder en la Argentina*. Buenos Aires: Ediciones Cen, 1964.

Hagen, Everett E., *On the Theory of Social Change*. Homewood, Ill.: The Dorsey Press, Inc., 1962.

Hook, Sidney, *The Hero in History*. New York: The Humanities Press, 1943.

Illia, Arturo, "Mensaje Presidencial," *Diario de Sesiones Cámara de Senadores de la Nación*, May 1, 1966. Buenos Aires: Imprenta del Congreso de la Nación.

Johnson, John J., *The Military and Society in Latin America*. Stanford, Calif., Stanford University Press, 1964.

Johnson, Kenneth F., *El Espectro de la Ideología Política Argentina, Ensayos y Medidas*. Buenos Aires: [N.N.], 1967.

Kennedy, John J. *Catholicism, Nationalism, and Democracy in Argentina.* Notre Dame, Ind.: University of Notre Dame Press, 1958.

Lasswell, Harold D., and Daniel Lerner, eds. *World Revolutionary Elites, Studies in Coercive Ideological Movements.* Cambridge, Mass.: Massachusetts Institute of Technology Press, 1966.

Levene, Gustavo Gabriel, *et al., Presidentes Argentinos.* Buenos Aires: Compañia General Fabril, 1961.

Lasswell, Harold D., Daniel Lerner, and C. Easton Rothwell, *The Comparative Study of Elites.* Stanford: Stanford University Press, 1952.

Ley de Los Partidos Políticos, No. 16.652. Buenos Aires: Talleres Gráficos de la Dirección General del Boletín Oficial e Imprentas del Ministerio del Interior, 1965.

Lieuwen, Edwin, *Arms and Politics in Latin America.* New York: Frederick A. Praeger, Inc., 1965.

Lipset, Seymour Martin, *Political Man.* New York: Doubleday & Company, Inc., 1960.

———, and Aldo Solari, eds., *Elites in Latin America.* New York: Oxford University Press, 1967.

Lozada, Salvador María, *El Régimen de las Asociaciones Profesionales.* Buenos Aires: A. Peña Lillo, 1960.

Luna, Félix, *Diálogos con Frondizi.* Buenos Aires: Editorial Desarrollo, 1963.

———, *La Historia Argentina en Función de los Objetivos Nacionales.* Buenos Aires: Ediciones Cen, 1965.

———, *Los Caudillos,* Buenos Aires: Editorial Jorge Alvarez S.A., 1966.

Macridis, Roy C., and Bernard C. Brown, eds., *Comparative Politics, Notes and Readings.* Homewood, Ill.: The Dorsey Press, Inc., 1961.

Mafud, Julio, *Psicología de la Viveza Criolla,* 2d ed. Buenos Aires: Editorial Américalee, 1965.

Manual del Peronista. Buenos Aires: Partido Peronista, 1948.

Marianetti, Benito, *Argentina, Realidad y Perspectivas.* Buenos Aires: Editorial Platina, 1964.

Martínez, García, *La Inflación Argentina.* Buenos Aires: Guillermo Kraft Ltda., 1965.

McGann, Thomas F., *Argentina: The Divided Land.* Princeton, N.J.: D. Van Nostrand Company, Inc., 1966.

Meisel, James H., *The Myth of the Ruling Class: Gaetano Mosca and the "Elite."* Ann Arbor, Mich.: University of Michigan Press, 1958.

Meynaud, Jean, and Alain Lancelot. *Las Actitudes Políticas.* Buenos Aires: Editorial Universitaria de Buenos Aires, 1965.

Michels, Robert, *Political Parties,* trans., Eden and Cedar Paul. New York: Hearst's International Library Co., 1915.

Miguens, José Enrique, "Un Análisis del Fenómeno," in Paita, ed., *Argentina, 1930–1960,* Buenos Aires: Editorial SUR S.R.L., 1961.

Mills, C. Wright, *The Power Elite.* New York: Oxford University Press, 1959.

Morris, James O., *Elites, Intellectuals, and Consensus.* Ithaca, N.Y.: Cornell University, 1966.

Mosca, Gaetano, *The Ruling Class.* New York: McGraw-Hill, Inc., 1939.

Orsolini, Mario H., *Ejército Argentino y Crecimiento Nacional.* Buenos Aires: Ediciones Arayú, 1965.

———, *La Crisis del Ejército,* Buenos Aires: Ediciones Arayú, 1964.

Padgett, L. Vincent, *The Mexican Political System.* Boston: Houghton Mifflin, 1966.

Paita, ed., *Argentina, 1930–1960.* Buenos Aires: Editorial SUR S.R.L., 1961.

Pan, Luis, *Justo y Marx: El Socialismo en la Argentina.* Buenos Aires: Ediciones Monserrat, 1964.

Pareto, Vilfredo, *The Mind and Society,* Vol. III, trans. A. Bongiorno and A. Livingston, eds. New York: Harcourt, Brace & World, Inc., 1935.

Ponsioen, J. A., *The Analysis of Social Change Reconsidered: A Sociological Study.* S-Gravenhage, The Netherlands: Mouton and Co., 1962.

Quién es Quién en la Argentina, Biografías Contemporáneas, 7th ed., 1958–1959. Buenos Aires: Guillermo Kraft, Ltda., 1958.

Quién es Quién en la Argentina, Biografías Contemporáneas, 8th ed., 1963. Buenos Aires: Guillermo Kraft, Ltda, 1964.

Ramos, Jorge Abelardo, *Historia Política del Ejército Argentino.* Buenos Aires: A. Peña Lillo, 1959.

Rennie, Ysabel F., *The Argentine Republic.* New York: The Macmillan Company, 1945.

Romero, José Luis, *A History of Argentine Political Thought,* trans. Thomas F. McGann. Stanford, Calif.: Stanford University Press, 1963.

———, *Breve Historia de la Argentina.* Buenos Aires: Universitaria de Buenos Aires, 1965.

Sánchez, Victorio, *Cultura Nacional o Cultura Liberal.* Buenos Aires: Ediciones Arayú, 1963.

Sánchez Viamonte, Carlos, *Manual de Derecho Constitucional.* Buenos Aires: Editorial Kapelusz, 1956.

Sarmiento, Domingo F., "Life in the Argentine Republic: Civilization or Barbarism," trans. Mrs. Horace Mann, in Joseph R. Barager, ed., *Why Perón Came to Power.* New York: Alfred A. Knopf, Inc., 1968.

Scalabrini Ortiz, Raúl, *El Hombre Que Está Solo y Espera.* Buenos Aires: Editorial Plus Ultra, 1966.

Scobie, James R., *Argentina: A City and a Nation.* New York: Oxford University Press, 1964.

Scoble, Harry, "Leadership Hierarchies and Political Issues in a New England Town," in Morris Janowitz, ed., *Community Political Systems.* New York: The Free Press, 1961.

Scott, Robert E., *Mexican Government in Transition.* Urbana: University of Illinois Press, 1959.

Sebreli, Juan José, *Buenos Aires Vida Cotidiana y Alienación.* Buenos Aires: Ediciones Siglo Veinte, 1964.

Seligman, Lester G., *Leadership in a New Nation.* New York: Atherton Press, 1964.

Silvert, Kalman H., *The Conflict Society.* New York: American Universities Field Staff, Inc., 1966.

Snow, Peter G., *Argentine Radicalism: The History and Doctrine of the Radical Civic Union.* Iowa City: University of Iowa Press, 1965.

Sorokin, Pitirim A., and Walter A. Lunden, *Power and Morality: Who Shall Guard the Guardians?* Boston: Porter and Sargent, 1959.

Sueldo, Horacio, "Fuerzas Armadas," in Paita, ed., *Argentina 1930–1960.* Buenos Aires: Editorial SUR, S.R.L., 1961.

Whitaker, Arthur P., *Argentina.* Englewood Cliffs, N. J.: Prentice-Hall, Inc., 1964.

———, and David C. Jordan. *Nationalism in Contemporary Latin America.* New York: The Free Press, 1966.

B. ARTICLES

Bidart Campos, Germán J., "Fuerzas Políticas en el Régimen Constitucional Argentino," *Cuadernos del Sur,* Año II, (octubre de 1965).

Dahl, Robert, "A Critique of the Ruling Elite Model," *The American Political Science Review,* LII (June 1958), 463–469.

Easton, David, "An Approach to the Analysis of Political Systems," *World Politics,* IX (April 1957), 383–400.

Fernández, Julio, "The Nationalism Syndrome in Argentina," *Journal of Inter-American Studies*, VIII (October 1966), 551–564.

Fitzgibbon, Russell H., "Revolutions: Western Hemisphere," *South Atlantic Quarterly*, LV (July 1956), 263–279.

———, "What Price Latin American Armies," *Virginia Quarterly Review*, XXXVI (Autumn 1960), 517–532.

Grondona, Mariano, "Después de Mendoza," *Primera Plana*, Año IV (26 de abril de 1966), p. 7.

———, "Golpe o Legalidad?" *Atlantida* (abril de 1966), 18–25.

Harrison, John P., "The Confrontation with the Political University," *The Annals of the American Academy of Political and Social Science*, CCCXXXIV (March 1961), 74-83.

Hoopes, Paul R., "The Problem of Cross-National Comparisons: A Methodological Note on Social Research in Argentina," *Sociology and Social Research*, LIII (July 1969), 475–481.

"La CGT y el cambio de estructuras," *Dinamis*, Año XXI (1 de abril de 1965), 8–11.

Linares Quintana, Segundo V., "Interacción de los Grupos de Presión y los Partidos Políticos," *Revista Argentina de Ciencia Política*, Año I (enero–junio de 1960), 56–66.

Prewitt, Kenneth, "Political Socialization and Leadership Selection," *The Annals of the American Academy of Political and Social Science*, CCCLXI (September 1965), 96–111.

Romero, César Enrique, "Problemática del Partido Político," *Revista Argentina de Ciencia Política*, Año I (enero–junio de 1960), 67–81.

Seligman, L. G., "Elite Recruitment and Political Development," *The Journal of Politics*, XXVI (August 1964), 612–626.

"Sin Partidos Hacia Nuevos Partidos," *Análisis*, Año VI (11 de julio de 1966), 1710.

Singer, J. David, "Cosmopolitan Attitudes and International Relations Courses," *The Journal of Politics*, XXVII (May 1965), 318–319.

C. NEWSPAPERS AND PERIODICALS

Buenos Aires, Argentina: *Análisis*
Confirmado
Clarín
La Nación
La Prensa
Primera Plana
Los Angeles, Calif.: *The Los Angeles Times*
New York, N. Y.: *The New York Times*

INDEX